Smart Soapmaking Around the Year
An Almanac of Projects, Experiments, and Investigations for Advanced Soap Making

— Anne L. Watson —

In between writing several of today's most popular and innovative beginner books on soapmaking—including the modern classics *Smart Soapmaking* and *Milk Soapmaking*—Anne L. Watson engaged in a number of projects, experiments, and investigations into areas of advanced soapmaking. A lot of it never got into those books!

Now Anne shares with you her explorations into such topics as herbal soaps, chocolate soaps, silk soaps, sea soaps, "wood" soaps, citrus soaps, cucumber soaps, oatmeal soaps, egg soaps, beer and wine soaps, castile soap, and even laundry soap. Along the way, she shares hard-earned tips about soap equipment and ingredients, choosing soapmaking suppliers, designing and resizing recipes, troubleshooting, trace accelerants, soda ash, essential oils and fragrances, natural colorants, gift soaps, and soapmaking as a business. And as a special bonus, she provides a fun and instructive look at the history of soap ads, using antique trade cards from her personal collection.

Looking for new challenges as a soapmaker? Anne's soapmaking almanac will keep you busy, engaged, and entertained throughout the year.

Anne L. Watson is the author of *Smart Soapmaking*, *Milk Soapmaking*, three more books on making soap and lotion, other popular books on home crafts and lifestyle, and many novels and children's books. In a previous career, she was a historic preservation architecture consultant. Anne lives in Bellingham, Washington. Please visit her at **www.annelwatson.com**.

Smart Soapmaking Around the Year

An Almanac of Projects,
Experiments, and Investigations
for Advanced Soap Making

Anne L. Watson

Next River Books
Bellingham, Washington

Author Online!

For updates and more resources,
visit Anne's Soapmaking Page at

www.annelwatson.com/soapmaking

Text and non-historic photos copyright © 2023, 2025 by Anne L. Watson
Portrait of Anne and Skeeter by Wendy Edelson
Victorian trade cards and other paper ephemera come from Anne's personal collection. Permission is granted to copy or reprint portions for any noncommercial use, except they may not be posted online without permission.

Version 1.3

Contents

JANUARY—SEA SOAPS ~ 9
Sea Products in Soapmaking—Why? ~ 10
Salt Soap ~ 10
Seaweed Soaps ~ 12
100% Coconut Oil Soap ~ 13
Sand Soap ~ 14
Classic Soap Ads—Sapolio ~ 15
What Would I Do? ~ 16
Soap Equipment—Tips and Tricks ~ 16
Soap Ingredients FAQ ~ 21
Soaps from the Past—Aleppo Soap ~ 22

FEBRUARY—CHOCOLATE SOAPS ~ 23
Chocolate in Soapmaking—Why? ~ 24
Kinds of Chocolate for Soapmaking ~ 25
Cocoa Butter as a Soapmaking Fat ~ 25
Using Chocolate Products in Soapmaking ~ 26
Do Chocolate Scent and Color Survive? ~ 29
Dark Chocolate Soap ~ 29
Cocoa Butter Soap ~ 30
Chocolate Coconut Soap ~ 30
Chocolate-ish Soap ~ 31
Chocolate Scents ~ 32
Vanilla and Discoloring ~ 32
What Would I Do? ~ 33
Resizing a Soap Recipe ~ 33
Soaps from the Past—Marseille Soap ~ 34

MARCH—LAUNDRY SOAP ~ 37
Homemade Laundry Soap—Why? ~ 38
Ingredients for Homemade Laundry Soap ~ 38
Basic Laundry Soap #1 ~ 40
Basic Laundry Soap #2 ~ 40
Grating Soap ~ 41
Soaps from the Past—Laundry the Old Way ~ 42
Castile Soap—Why? ~ 46
Castile Soap Experiments ~ 46
Easy Castile Soap with Variations ~ 48
Increasing Lather ~ 49
Dog Soap ~ 51
What Would I Do? ~ 51
Soaps from the Past—Historical Castile Soap ~ 52

APRIL—EGG SOAPS ~ 53
Eggs in Soapmaking—Why? ~ 54
Egg Yolk Soap ~ 55
Swedish Egg White Soap ~ 56
Cool Whole Egg Soap ~ 57
Does Egg Soap Spoil Quickly? ~ 58
Designing Soaps for Different Uses ~ 58
Analyzing and Fixing Problems ~ 59
Soaps from the Past—Additives in Soap ~ 61

MAY—SILK SOAPS ~ 65
Silk in Soapmaking—Why? ~ 66
Using Silk in Soapmaking ~ 66
Using Floral Scents ~ 67
Flowers-and-Silk Soap ~ 69
Floral Soap with Coconut Milk ~ 70
Using Fruit Fragrances ~ 71
Soaps from the Past—Wild, Weird, and Wonderful Soap Ads ~ 72

JUNE—CUCUMBER SOAPS ~ 91
Cucumbers in Soapmaking—Why? ~ 92
Avoiding Burned Cucumber Odor ~ 92
Basic Cucumber Soap and Variations ~ 93
Cucumber and Apricot Soap ~ 94
Cucumber and Avocado Soap ~ 94
Color—Natural and Artificial ~ 95
Hardness ~ 95
Does Cucumber Accelerate Trace? ~ 95
What Would I Do? ~ 96
Low Temperature Soapmaking ~ 96

JULY—CITRUS SOAPS ~ 99
Citrus in Soapmaking—Why? ~ 100
Fading and Citrus Essential Oils ~ 101
Basic Citrus Soap and Variations ~ 101
Texas Ruby Red Grapefruit Soap ~ 103
Lemongrass, Coconut, and Almond Soap ~ 104
Creamy Orange Soap ~ 105
What Would I Do? ~ 106
Soapmaking as a Business ~ 106

AUGUST—HERBAL SOAPS ~ 109
Herbs in Soapmaking—Why? ~ 110
Botanicals in Soap ~ 111
Infusing Oils with Herbs ~ 111
Herb Teas ~ 112
Herb Essential Oils and Fragrances ~ 112
Botanicals and Lye ~ 114
Basic Herbal Soap and Variations ~ 115
Coconut Almond Soap with Herb Tea ~ 117
Triple Calendula Soap ~ 118
Tomato Basil Soap ~ 119
Lavender, Shea, and Almond Soap ~ 120
Working with Accelerants ~ 121
What Would I Do? ~ 122

SEPTEMBER—OATMEAL SOAPS ~ 123
Oatmeal in Soapmaking—Why? ~ 124
Rolled Oats and Oat Flour ~ 125
Honey and Beeswax ~ 125
Liquids—Milk, Cream, and Oat Milk ~ 126
Cinnamon and Other Spices ~ 127
Oatmeal, Milk, and Honey Fragrance Oils ~ 127
Basic Oatmeal Soap and Variations ~ 128
Oatmeal, Wheat Germ, and Buttermilk Soap ~ 129
What Would I Do? ~ 130
Selecting Vendors ~ 131

OCTOBER—BEER AND WINE SOAPS ~ 133
Beer and Wine in Soapmaking—Why? ~ 134
Experimenting—Why? ~ 134
Using Alcoholic Beverages in Soapmaking ~ 135
Basic Beer Soap and Variations ~ 137
All-Veg Beer Soap ~ 138
Trying Wine in Soapmaking ~ 139
Wine Soap Experiments and Recipes ~ 140
What Would I Do? ~ 143
Developing Your Own Recipes ~ 143
An Approach to Experimenting ~ 146

NOVEMBER—NATURAL COLORANTS ~ 147

Natural Colorants in Soapmaking—Why? ~ 148
Using Natural Colorants in Soapmaking ~ 149
Colors, Oils, and Soap ~ 150
Plant-Based Colorants ~ 151
Other Natural Colorants ~ 154
Basic Colored Soap #1 ~ 155
Basic Colored Soap #2 ~ 157
Alkanet Root Soap Experiment ~ 158
Madder Root Soap Experiment ~ 159
Pumpkin Pie Soap ~ 161
What Would I Do? ~ 162
Taming the Soda Ash Monster ~ 162

DECEMBER—WOOD SOAPS ~ 165

Wood Scents in Soapmaking—Why? ~ 166
Evergreen and Other Tree Essential Oils ~ 167
Sandalwood EO vs. FO—Is the Difference Worth the Cost? ~ 167
Basic Wood Soap and Variations ~ 168
Soaps from the Past—Pine Tar Soap ~ 168
Easy Pine Tar Soap ~ 169
What Would I Do? ~ 170
Fragrances and Essential Oils for Gift Soaps ~ 171
Holiday Fragrance Oils ~ 171
Gift Soap in a Hurry ~ 172
Packaging Soaps for Gifts ~ 173
Giving a Soapmaking Lesson ~ 174
Shaving Soap ~ 175
Home Fragrancing ~ 177

Before We Begin

Soap is a yardstick of civilization.

—Sigmund Freud

I'm not sure I'd go *that* far. But soapmaking *is* a very ancient craft—and like many traditions, it's complex.

Almost any kind of soap will get you clean. But beyond that, what do we look for? There are so many things to consider—lather, fragrance, color, and effects on the skin, to name just a few.

Then there's the whole process of *making* that soap. Is it easy or tricky? How long does the soap need to age before it's safe and pleasant to use?

What additives are beneficial? Which affect the chemistry of the process? How can we get around difficulties?

How do you turn soapmaking into a business, if that's what you want?

This almanac started life as a monthly "magazine" posted on my web site, where I shared projects, experiments, and investigations I took up between writing my first three books on soap and lotion making. There was a lot that never got into the books!

Along with practical questions, I gave some attention to the social and cultural side of soap—to attitudes and prejudices and myths. I'm fascinated by soap advertising and its claims, and by the history of the daily process of cleaning ourselves, our homes, and our clothing. All of that says a lot about where we've been, and maybe something about where we're going.

I'm glad now to offer all this in the more enduring form of an almanac—something to keep in your collection of soapmaking references.

Before we start, though, here are just a few practical notes:

Most important, this is *not* a beginning soapmaker's "how-to" book. It contains many recipes, but they're mostly just ingredients lists, because I assume you already know how to make soap. If you do need basic directions, please see one or more of my other books—especially *Smart Soapmaking* and *Milk Soapmaking*—or any other reputable resource.

Just as in my earlier books, each recipe makes a 30-ounce batch, unless I say otherwise.

For most months, you'll find a section called "What Would I Do?" That's my corner for preferences, opinions, and editorializing. Just look for this icon:

JANUARY

SEA SOAPS

Soap Equipment and Ingredients

Sea Products in Soapmaking—Why?

Though I haven't found any evidence of traditional use of seaweed in soaps, there are many modern versions. Many of them make claims of exfoliating, melting fat, or feeding the skin—but whether they do or not is debatable. Salt soaps too are described as exfoliating, which is easy to believe.

Silica (sand) soap was sold as "scouring soap" in the nineteenth and early twentieth centuries.

The main reasons for making soaps with sea products would probably be esthetics and customer demand.

There are many "sea" fragrance oils, but I have yet to find one that doesn't smell like laundry detergent.

Salt Soap

I was surprised that this salt soap isn't gritty or scrubby. It has a smooth texture, and the lather is thick and creamy. However, I found it very drying.

> 24 ounces (680 grams) coconut oil
> 3 ounces (85 grams) olive oil
> 1.5 ounces (43 grams) grapeseed oil
> 1.5 ounces (43 grams) refined wheat germ oil
> 10.5 ounces (298 grams) water
> 4.8 ounces (136 grams) lye
> 30 ounces (851 grams) sea salt

Use non-iodized kosher salt or sea salt. Avoid Dead Sea salt, which contains many other minerals and tends to ooze when used in soap.

Melt the coconut oil and combine with the liquid fats. Dissolve the lye in the water. Add the lye solution to the combined fats and blend until well emulsified or at light trace. Add the salt and stir it in well by hand. Pour into molds.

If you use a single block mold, cut as soon as the soap hardens. Made in a block, salt soaps are likely to chip at the bottom of each cut when you slice them. If possible with your soap cutter, cut the block partway through, rotate it 180 degrees, and cut down to meet the first cuts. Or make a very shallow cut, just enough to mark the soap, and rotate the block 90 degrees—that way, you'll have guide lines for where to do the next cut. Cutting precisely on those lines, cut about a third of the way through. Rotate 90 degrees again, and complete the cut. Since there isn't a "bottom" to chip out, you should be able to avoid chips. Wear gloves while you're doing this. Salt soaps harden so quickly, the soap may still be somewhat caustic when it's time to cut it.

Or make it in a tray mold with dividers. If you use this option, line the bottom of the tray mold before pouring the soap in.

Or make the soap in individual molds. To discourage crumbling at the bottom and corners of the bars, freeze the molds for 15 minutes before removing the soaps.

Individually molded soaps made with kosher salt (white), Himalayan pink salt, and black Hawaiian salt. The colors tended to fade over time.

The soaps in the photo above are nice for color samples, but the molds are far too small and irregular in shape to make good soaps. For a fun experiment, I tried suspending them in clear melt-and-pour soap. I enhanced several of the shells with soap paint and suspended them in clear M&P in a round mold. The melted soap base did remove some of the soap paint, but results were attractive.

Seaweed Soaps

Various seaweeds, from an antique encyclopedia

Not everyone likes the smell of seaweed in soap! It's often described as fishy. Others love it—but start with a very small batch if you want to experiment. Essential oils such as eucalyptus and rosemary are often recommended for use with seaweed.

Seaweed adds some color to soap, but the color may fade as the soap cures.

Don't add large chunks of seaweed to soap. They tend to get slimy in use.

Here are a few types of seaweed you can use in soapmaking:

Kelp—Produces a dark green color. Has a strong scent that fades somewhat as the soap cures. The amount you use makes a big difference in how strongly the soap smells. About 1½ teaspoons would be the maximum for one of my 30-ounce recipes. Add at trace.

Spirulina—Produces a dark green color, and has a lasting scent. The color may fade. For my typical 30-ounce recipe, I'd use about a half teaspoon of spirulina powder. Add at trace.

Nori—A seaweed wrap used in sushi. It's crumbled into tiny bits and added to soap at trace, or infused in the oils or the essential oils. Or it may be cooked and added as a puree.

Seaweeds, left to right: kelp, spirulina, nori

100% Coconut Oil Soap

Coconut oil soap is supposedly the only kind that will lather in salt water. I mentioned this to a commercial fisherman I know, and he looked at me like I'd lost my mind. "No one would bathe in the sea," he said. Maybe not. Or maybe, if you're cruising around the world in a small sailboat, you do? In any event, the soap has fine lather. It's superfatted at 20%, so it's not drying.

> 30 ounces (851 grams) coconut oil
> 9 ounces (255 grams) water
> 4.4 ounces (125 grams) lye

Although it doesn't trace that quickly, the soap sets and hardens very fast. It's a good choice for complex 3-D molds, such as the ones I used for the soaps in the photo. These were made without fragrance or other additives, so they're pure white. (It would be interesting to make them with natural colorants.)

Some soapmakers also use 100% coconut oil soap for salt bars. If you choose to do this, add 30 ounces of sea salt to the recipe. See the salt soap recipe above for comments about mixing, molds, and slicing.

Coconut Milk Variation—Substitute frozen coconut milk for the water. Proceed as for milk soap.

Sand Soap

    I was intrigued when a friend told me about sand soap. I decided to try it in the coconut oil recipe because coconut oil soap sets very quickly, which I suspected would be helpful in keeping the sand from all sinking to the bottom.
    Add the sand at trace, and keep stirring until the mixture reaches heavy trace.
    You can also do this with suspending melt and pour soap base.
    I used fine, sanitized sand that's intended for reptile terrariums. With sand this fine and soft, you get a scrub bar. With a coarser sand, it might be used like a pumice block, for heavy exfoliation on feet or other heavy callouses.
    I wouldn't just scoop some up from the beach. How much to use depends on how much exfoliation you want—I used 4 tablespoons of sand per pound of oils.

Cold process soap made with fine sand

Classic Soap Ads—Sapolio

Speaking of scouring soaps, here's a very funny ad for Sapolio, an early commercial soap of this type.

Parson Wilder Calls on Mrs. Puffy.
By Neil Burgess.

"It did my soul good," said Mrs. Puffy, "to see Old Parson Wilder come in, the dear old soul; he looked as smiling as a basket of chips, and it was a nice morning, the sun shining right into our setting-room; and, as luck would have it, I'd just got all cleaned up and had put on a clean calico and white apron, and, if I do say it, I looked as slick as a whistle; and our garden — well, you'd oughter to seen it — a mass of posies and blossoms everywhere; and as it had rained in the night, everything was as fresh as a cowcumber. 'Well, well!' says the parson, 'this is a picture one could never forget,' and he looked at my floor and kitchen-

able; they were both white as snow, and my milk-pans — well, you could just see your face in em, and everything was as neat as a pink.

"I cut him a pie and got him a pitcher of milk, 'cause I could see he was powerful hungry, and when he got filled up he commenced: 'Cleanliness is next to godliness; now,' says he, 'what makes this home look so bright and pure as the lily?' Says I. 'It's Sapolio.'

"'How?' says he, putting his hand to his ear, 'cause he's a little deaf. 'Sapolio!' I yelled in his ear. 'No,' says he, 'no; it's virtoo, moral virtoo, that's er shining through it all,' and he kept that up till supper-time, and stayed and eat a big supper (I'm afraid they ain't er feeding the old man as well up to his house as they oughter); and after he had gone hum, I couldn't help thinking, as I looked at my floor, table, pans and etceterer, that it may be moral virtoo shining through 'em, *but it takes Sapolio to fetch it out!*"

If your grocer does not keep Sapolio, he can order it for you from any wholesale grocer in the United States.

What is Sapolio?

It is a solid, handsome cake of scouring soap, which has no equal for all cleaning purposes, except the laundry.

What will Sapolio do? Why, it will clean paint, make oil-cloths bright. You can scour the knives and forks with it, and make the tin things shine brightly.

The wash-basin, the bath-tub, even the greasy kitchen sink, will be as clean as a new pin if you use **SAPOLIO**.

BEWARE OF IMITATIONS.

What Would I Do?

I don't think I'd use black or pink salt in soap again. The color didn't seem stable enough in soap. Actually, I don't think I'd make salt soap at all for my own use—I found it very drying.

What I *do* plan to do again is make 100% coconut oil soap. I think I'll adopt that one for hand soap for my house. Love the lather!

Soap Equipment—Tips and Tricks

I have contact information in my books, and there are a few questions I get repeatedly. This is just a summary of my answers to frequently asked questions—*not* a listing of *all* the things you need. Also, keep in mind that these are my own ideas and preferences. You really need to think about this for your own work, and take or leave anyone else's ideas according to what you decide is right for you.

Goggles

Glasses aren't good enough—however, if you wear glasses, you'll need goggles that fit over your glasses. Also—and this is really important—you must have either fog-proof goggles, or a cloth or cleaner or some other treatment that keeps the lenses from fogging. Because otherwise, you're all but blind—and if you have glasses as well as goggles, completely so. Sometimes these non-fogging goggles and treatments can be found in shops that sell motorcycle gear.

Test whatever you plan to use for soapmaking. Use your goggles and glasses for a cooking task, or wear them when you open your dishwasher at the end of a cycle. Or even just wear them for a while. The last thing you need is for your eye protection to start causing problems while you're making soap.

Gloves

I use dishwashing gloves that are smaller than I'd use for housecleaning or dishwashing. The glove should preserve your dexterity—it's important to not be clumsy.

Shoes

Solid shoes will protect your feet if you spill something. I've never spilled anything, but I always wear them anyway.

Masks

I've tried masks and respirators, and found them only marginally helpful. They didn't compensate for poor ventilation.

Other Clothing

I've used a lab coat, and found it too hot. Another alternative would be a liquid-proof dishwashing apron. Whatever clothing you use, spend a few minutes considering how quickly you could get out of it, if something were to splash on it. Liquid spreads on absorbent fabrics, so a cloth bib apron might keep you from removing a long sleeved shirt as quickly as you otherwise could.

Scales and Weighing

It's tempting to go for more and more accurate scales. Actually, one that is accurate to one gram or one-tenth of an ounce is fine. I use a power supply cord to avoid possible problems with batteries.

Subtractive Weighing—I figured out a handy weighing trick, though it may not work with all scales. When you're weighing solid ingredients such as shea butter, put the whole container of shea butter on the scale and tare the scale. Then, using a spoon, start removing shea butter into your heating container. If you want 30 grams of shea butter, remove until your scale reads minus thirty grams.

Heating and Melting Equipment

I use a microwave oven for melting most solid fats. They can also be melted in a low oven (using a water bath around the container), *carefully* on the stovetop (in a double boiler), or in any number of small electric warming devices, from mug warmers to bread proofers. Just be aware that fats can cause serious fires, and be careful.

I keep beeswax in a mason jar and melt it in a yogurt maker or slow cooker with a rack and water in the bottom. (This takes much longer than a microwave, so you have to think of this well in advance.) I use the subtractive weighing technique I described just above to remove the amount of beeswax I need, using a plastic spoon. Beeswax can be very hard to remove from things, so I like to avoid any need to do it.

Pots

Stainless steel is the material of choice—but you *don't* want high-grade stainless steel cookware. Gourmet pots usually have heat-distributing cores in the bottom—which is exactly what you don't want for soap. Thin pots, pots you'd never cook in, are best. I got mine at the local hardware store. Thrift stores are also a good source. A good soapmaking pot should be cheap, for a stainless steel pot, but make very sure it is stainless. It should say "stainless" or "INOX" on the bottom. You can also test with a magnet, but some stainless isn't magnetic. So, if it does attract the magnet, it's definitely not aluminum, but if it doesn't, you still don't know. Play this one safe—aluminum plus lye is very bad.

I had an idea that a smaller diameter pot would work better for smaller batches, but it didn't. For some reason, the small diameter caused a lot of suction between the stick blender and the pot bottom. Making soap was a real struggle, and I went back to my old soup pot, tipping it to keep the stick blender submerged.

Thermometers

Thermometers are very helpful when you're learning. You don't need an expensive one. A waterproof digital instant-read food thermometer is just fine. The one I use for teaching costs less than $15.

Once you know exactly what trace looks like, you probably will never need a thermometer again. It's a learning tool, that's all.

Remote infrared thermometers are a waste of money for soap. They cost a lot and don't last long under soapmaking conditions.

Stick Blenders

My first stick blender was one I picked up at a thrift store. It worked OK.

When I was just finishing one of my books—I think it was *Milk Soapmaking*—the silly thing tanked. I had to run off and get a new stick blender in a hurry, and the thrift store didn't have any. Annoyed, I bought a fairly pricey one at a department store. Pricey was all they had.

I got home and went back to making my soap. The difference between the new stick blender and the old one was unbelievable. It really is worth getting a good one.

Countertop Blenders

I wish they were bigger! They're much easier to use than a stick blender, with less fumes and more thorough mixing. I think they're faster, too.

Larger commercial ones are available, but they cost more than I'm willing to pay. So, I use my countertop blender for my small test batches.

If you want to use a countertop blender, I recommend one with a glass container, especially if you're planning to use it for anything but soapmaking. Plastic works, but the blender jar becomes frosted from soapmaking. I have a blender with a six-cup container, and it will handle slightly under one pound oil weight of soap—which makes about four bars.

Experiment with your blender before using it for soap—find out its maximum liquid capacity by testing with water. You can't fill them to the top—they will overflow when you turn them on.

Electric Mixers

You can use a heavy stand mixer for fairly small soap batches. Use a paddle attachment, if there is one—otherwise you'll be mixing lots of air into the soap. On the other hand, there's nothing particularly wrong with floating soap. Ivory made a name for themselves with it.

Two big caveats: You *must* use a spatter shield for the bowl. And you must, must, must make sure there's no aluminum where the raw soap will touch it. Use a magnet to test every part of your mixer. If a magnet doesn't stick to any of the metal pieces, don't use that mixer around soap.

Stand mixers are used for whipped soap, with some beautiful results.

Molds

I prefer silicone molds—it's so much easier to remove the soap. And you can put them in the dishwasher. Most can even be used for CPOP, although it's a good idea to ask the vendor about temperature. One consideration with silicone molds and CPOP, though—a wood mold will hold the warmth much longer after you turn your oven off, so may be more effective.

However, I have bought one silicone mold that smelled absolutely horrible, like toxic waste. And several that were pictured online in such a way as to make you think the soaps were reasonable-sized—only to find they were about the size of a single grape. I'm not sure what molds of this kind are for—possibly decorative add-ons for candles? Regardless, they're often mislabeled as soap molds, and even when they're basically nice, they're not soap molds.

Another issue with silicone baking molds is color leaching. I've had this only with red molds that were intended for baking use rather than specifically for soap.

Soap with bleeding color from red silicone mold

One silicone mold—and this one was sold by a reputable company as a soap mold—sort of melded into the soap. Once the soap had set, there was no actual point where the soap ended and the mold began. There was soap on top, grading into a substance that resembled tile caulk, and the outside of the mess still looked like normal silicone. I had to throw the whole thing away. (They are no longer selling this item.)

Be aware that not all shapes make good soap. Many of the shell shapes I show here aren't really a good choice for molds, interesting as they may be for color samples. I'm no fan of soaps that are impractical, including those that are "too pretty to use."

pH Testing

I recommend pH papers, and they must be able to show values at least from 7 to 14. It doesn't matter if they can also show values below 7, but it doesn't help anything, either. pH papers will NOT give you exact pH information. What they will do is let you know if you have very high pH, either overall or in spots. I test a spot or two on most batches, and much more if anything looks unusual.

The last time I tried a pH meter, it didn't work well. I contacted the manufacturer, who told me that inexpensive pH meters *don't* work well for soap. Whether that's still true, I don't know. But I wouldn't spend money on one again, unless I was sure it would work.

Saving Money on Equipment

It's not unlikely that you can find a great stainless steel pot at a thrift store. And, as also mentioned above, you don't need an especially high-quality thermometer. Inexpensive pH papers work better than pH meters. I've also found silicone muffin pans and loaf pans on thrift store shelves. As well as rubber spatulas, spoons, and other cooking gear.

All kinds of found objects can be used for soap molds, from reusable-disposable food containers—sold as "Gladware" and under other trade names in the wrap and bag aisle of most supermarkets—to the quart-size milk cartons I mention in *Smart Soapmaking*.

Soapmaking books usually show glass measuring cups used for weighing containers, but unless the container will be heated, it's fine to use old peanut butter jars, or any other ordinary jar with a mouth that's wide enough to be practical. If a container will be heated, a mason jar works perfectly—and thrift stores often have them by the dozen.

I'm asked many times if I reuse my cooking equipment for soapmaking. I do—EXCEPT for plastics, which pick up fragrance. If glass or stainless steel equipment is cleaned properly, it is perfectly safe to use for both cooking and soapmaking.

Cleaning Your Equipment

It's a big, big exception for me to mention a brand name—but in this case, I will. Of all the washing methods I've tried, this is the best:

Using NO water, squirt Blue Dawn dishwashing liquid onto the surfaces of your pots and utensils. Work up a lather with a dishwashing brush. Then rinse thoroughly. If you have a dishwasher, run the soapmaking equipment in a regular load with dishwasher detergent. If not, repeat the hand wash treatment once.

It helps a lot to have a stick blender with a detachable blade that can go in the dishwasher. For the initial cleaning, though, run the stick blender for a minute in a container of clear, warm water. This helps clean the back sides of the blades, which can be hard to keep free of soap and scale.

If you use a countertop blender, fill the jar about a quarter full with clean water after the soap is poured. Run it for half a minute or so. Then dump the water, disassemble the blender, and wash each piece separately or in the dishwasher.

Soap Ingredients FAQ

Here are the questions I've been asked over and over about ingredients.

* * *

Is "almond oil" the same thing as "sweet almond oil"?
Yes. Bitter almond oil exists, but it's rare and will be specially labeled.

* * *

Should I use refined or unrefined shea butter? What about other fats?
Depends what you want. Unrefined shea butter and many other unrefined fats have scents of their own. The scent of various batches of unrefined shea butter varies but can be straw-like, walnut-like, or even smoky. I recommend it for use with fairly sturdy, not-sweet scents, such as musk, amber, patchouli, or sweetgrass. For a delicate floral scent, I'd use refined.

Unrefined wheat germ oil smells strongly like vitamin pills. Refined is much better.

Other unrefined oils have more or less scent, and the best plan would be to try a small amount from your chosen vendor and see whether it works for your use.

Unrefined oils often have more color, too, which may be desirable or not, depending on the look you want.

* * *

Should I use extra-virgin olive oil?
No. It's a waste of money to use fine olive oil in soap. In fact, less expensive olive oil often works better—it's less expensive because it doesn't have the fine olive scent that the good stuff does. Olive scent is great in salad dressing, but who wants to wash with it?

Also, extra-virgin olive oil is sometimes adulterated. I haven't heard of any cases of adulteration with inexpensive olive oil—probably it's not worth their trouble.

* * *

Is pomace better than other olive oil? Does it saponify faster?
As far as I've ever noticed, no and no.

* * *

Does shea butter accelerate trace? Is it true that you can't use shea for more than a small percentage of the fats?
I've heard over and over that shea accelerates trace, but have never experienced it. I've made lots of soap that's one-third shea butter. When I was in the soap business, someone told my partner one day, "You can't make soap with more than 10% shea butter." She looked around at our stock and said thoughtfully, "Oooohhh. Wonder what all this stuff is, then…"

* * *

Is grocery store coconut oil the same as "76 degree coconut oil"? What about 92 degree coconut oil? Fractionated coconut oil? Virgin coconut oil?

Grocery store coconut oil is the same as 76 degree coconut oil.

92 degree coconut oil is hydrogenated. I've never used it.

Fractionated coconut oil is a liquid that's different from any other type of coconut oil. You can't substitute in recipes.

Virgin coconut oil is unrefined 76 degree coconut oil. It's more expensive, and its coconut odor may be lost in saponification.

* * *

What kind of lye do you recommend?

For general use, bead lye. It must be 100% sodium hydroxide. In some states you can get it in hardware stores and grocery stores. In others, you can't.

Microbead lye is great for use with cold mixtures, but it's much more likely to scatter or be moved in an air current than bead lye is. I wouldn't recommend it for beginners.

I don't care for flake lye, and definitely don't recommend it for cold mixtures. It's somewhat easier to handle, but it's much harder to dissolve.

Soaps from the Past—Aleppo Soap

Aleppo soap is one of the oldest of the traditional soaps. It is made from a combination of olive oil and bay fruit oil. Bay fruit is the berry of the bay laurel tree, and the oil is not the same as bay laurel essential oil, which is distilled from the leaves.

Up to 30% of the oil is bay fruit oil, the rest is olive. Traditionally, the soap is produced by a lengthy industrial hot process.

Bay fruit oil is difficult to find in small quantities. The soap is hard and long lasting, but the sample I bought wasn't particularly exceptional in terms of aesthetic appeal. It's not one I'd go to great lengths to make.

FEBRUARY

CHOCOLATE SOAPS

Resizing a Soap Recipe

Chocolate in Soapmaking—Why

Valentine trade card for Laird's Bloom of Youth and White Lilac Soap

Other than personal preference, the reason for making chocolate soap would be mostly marketability. It would probably be a seasonal or gift-type product, and it seems to sell better in some markets than in others.

Variations on chocolate soap—such as chocolate mint, chocolate cherry, or chocolate orange—may be especially attractive. It's important for the soaps to have a strong chocolate scent—customers will sniff before they buy. Guest soap sizes of chocolate soap may be marketable as a novelty item, as they look very much like chocolate candy.

One caveat: Chocolate products in soap may create brown drips or residue in the shower or tub. They may also make dark lather that could stain linens.

Chocolate fragrances cause strong discoloration, which may also result in a dark lather. Lather that stains can be mostly avoided by marbling chocolate soap into a lighter colored batch—but then you probably lose the chocolate scent, or most of it.

Cocoa butter soaps have a lovely, silky texture and don't have the staining problem. They do have a mild chocolate fragrance. However, cocoa butter can clog pores and contribute to acne. If this might be an issue at all, chocolate soaps are probably best used as hand soaps rather than facial soaps.

Kinds of Chocolate for Soapmaking

There's a wealth of chocolate products to choose from:

- baking chocolate
- cocoa powder
- chocolate chips
- white chocolate
- semi-sweet/bittersweet chocolate
- chocolate milk
- cocoa butter

And a few that it may be wise to avoid:

- candy melts
- chocolate candy
- chocolate syrup
- any product with unknown percentages of different fats
- chocolate with a higher-than-normal content of cocoa solids (such as 80% cocoa)

Cocoa Butter as a Soapmaking Fat

The fat in chocolate is cocoa butter, which makes a smooth, hard soap with good creamy lather. Of course, cocoa butter soap doesn't have to look or smell like chocolate. Cocoa butter is available in a deodorized form, if the chocolate scent isn't wanted. It is pale colored, so it doesn't make a soap with dark lather.

Expensive if bought in small quantities, cocoa butter is sold by soapmaking supply vendors for reasonable prices.

There is a myth that cocoa butter can only be used for a small percentage of a soap formulation. That's what it is, nothing but a myth. As long as your hardness and lather numbers work out, there's no reason not to use larger amounts.

To increase the chocolate character without affecting the lather, you could add cocoa powder, first sifting it and then stick blending it thoroughly with one of the oils. Add at trace. I'd use about one teaspoon of cocoa to each pound of base oils.

You could also mix chocolate fragrance with a little of the soap batter and swirl it in. Since chocolate fragrance will not color the soap immediately, you would probably get a better swirl if you use colorant as well.

Using Chocolate Products in Soapmaking

1884 ad for Baker's Cocoa and Chocolate

Since I have access to ingredients only in the United States, my calculations are based on US food labeling and ingredients laws.

There is plenty of information on food labels, but be careful of column headings when you use food labels. The "nutrition information" can be somewhat confusing, with fat percentages expressed in terms of daily average recommended dietary amounts instead of being a percentage of product weight.

Most soapmakers use cocoa or unsweetened baking chocolate for soapmaking. Other possible forms of chocolate are white chocolate, bittersweet chocolate, chocolate milk, and chocolate chips.

Many soapmakers treat the chocolate as an additive and don't figure it in the lye calculation. Typically, chocolate will be added to some of the soap batter at trace and mixed into the rest of the soap just before pouring. This works, especially if the superfatting of the formulation is low enough to absorb the extra fat. If I were going to ignore the fat in chocolate products, I'd limit superfatting to 5%. You can use a higher percentage of chocolate if you do calculate the cocoa butter as part of the fats.

Some soapmakers swirl melted chocolate into the soap at trace, but I did not try this.

If you want to calculate the chocolate as part of the fats, begin by looking at the ingredient label. It really isn't possible to do a calculation if there is a mixture of fats in the product, although I'd ignore minor amounts of milk fat. But, unless another fat is specified, the fat in the product is cocoa butter.

Unsweetened Chocolate Products

Baking Chocolate

Bitter chocolate should be around 50% cocoa butter. The rest is cocoa solids.

Use like any other solid fat. Calculate it as cocoa butter, but use double the amount of chocolate.

When melting baking chocolate, be aware that it can melt almost completely without losing its solid shape. Don't overheat.

Or superfat the soap at no more than 5% and ignore the cocoa butter in the chocolate in your lye calculation. This works fine as long as the chocolate quantity is a fairly small percentage of the soap ingredients.

Cocoa Powder

The cocoa butter content varies with brand, as do other ingredients. With US labeling, the ingredient label will list the number of grams of fat in 1 tablespoon of cocoa powder. One tablespoon of cocoa powder weighs about 7.4 grams. So, if there's .5 grams of fat in 1 tablespoon of cocoa powder, as there is in one popular brand, it's about 1/15 fat. This is probably negligible. Some brands will contain 20% fat, and that might be worth calculating.

There are two types of cocoa powder—natural and Dutch process. The natural type is more acidic. This affects baking, but probably doesn't make enough difference to matter in soapmaking.

Always sift cocoa before using, and mix it carefully with the other ingredients—it has a tendency to lump. Cocoa is usually used at the rate of one teaspoon of cocoa per pound of oils.

There are several ways to mix cocoa into the soap. You can dissolve the cocoa in your liquid ingredient before making soap. It's necessary to dissolve cocoa in hot liquid, but it would have to be cooled or frozen before adding the lye.

Or withhold part of the water from the lye solution, dissolve the cocoa powder in that part of the liquid, and add at trace.

Or add the powder directly to the liquid fats, or to the soap mixture at trace. This could result in a scrub soap with gritty bits of cocoa in it. When I did it this way, it didn't produce a scrub soap, but I haven't experimented enough to say for sure that it never would. It might depend on the amount of cocoa you used.

Sweetened Chocolate Products

Sugar in a soap formulation will increase lather. It has to be handled carefully to prevent overheating and discoloration/scorching. It can also decrease time to trace. So, I use Cool Technique with these products. (That's explained in my books *Milk Soapmaking* and *Cool Soapmaking*.)

Chocolate chips, white chocolate, semi-sweet/bittersweet chocolate, and chocolate milk have varying amounts of sugar. If you figure the cocoa butter in the lye calculation, use the same method as for unsweetened chocolate. Melt solid chocolate products with the solid fats.

Chocolate Chips

These are around 40% cocoa butter. If you're using the fat content in your lye calculation, make sure the product contains no fat other than cocoa butter. Also, be aware of sugar content. It varies by brand, but a tablespoon of chocolate chips contains about 8 grams, or approximately 2 teaspoons, of sugar. This would be as much sugar as would be recommended for a two pound batch of soap, and it isn't a lot of chocolate. Check the ingredients list for any "wild card" ingredients that might affect soapmaking.

White Chocolate

In the US, this will contain at least 20% cocoa butter, as much as 55% sugar, milk solids, and some salt. Check the label for sugar content. Since the recommended amount of sugar in cold process soap is no more than 1 teaspoon (.147 ounce, or 4.2 grams) per pound of oils, you can get excess sugar in your soap fairly quickly with white chocolate, which can cause it to overheat.

Semi-Sweet and Bittersweet Chocolate

This will vary by brand. Check the sugar content, and also the cocoa solids. Baking chocolate, at approximately 50% cocoa solids, causes deposits of chocolate powder on the top surface of the soap. A lower percentage would be desirable, but many gourmet semi-sweet and bittersweet chocolate products boast a higher percentage—as much as 80%. I didn't experiment with such products, but would be surprised if they made good soap.

Chocolate milk

It doesn't contain enough chocolate to calculate. Substitute chocolate milk in any milk soap recipe. Most commercial chocolate milk is skim milk, so there's no addition to creaminess in the finished soap.

Valentine trade card from Curtis Davis & Company's Welcome Soap

Do Chocolate Scent and Color Survive?

Yes and no. In my experiments, neither the scent nor the color of some chocolate products survived saponification very well, while others remained strongly chocolate-y. *But when the chocolate content is strong enough that the soap has a strong chocolate character, you're likely to get brown lather as well.*

• Bitter baking chocolate retains its color and a surprising amount of chocolate scent. It makes a dark lather.

• Cocoa powder added to soap loses most or all of its scent. I've had batches where the color lasted, others where it didn't. Little if any color in the lather.

• White chocolate and commercial chocolate milk almost disappear into soap.

• Non-deodorized cocoa butter retains a chocolate fragrance. How well that comes through in soap depends on the percentage of cocoa butter, as well as any other oil odors in the blend.

Some soapmakers add chocolate to melt and pour soap. I haven't tried this, but the usual approach seems to be to add up to 1 tablespoon of cocoa powder per pound of soap base—often a cocoa butter soap base.

Dark Chocolate Soap

9 ounces (256 grams) baking chocolate
15 ounces (425 grams) coconut oil
10.5 ounces (298 grams) grapeseed oil
9 ounces (256 grams) water
4.4 ounces (127 grams) lye
1.2 ounces (34 grams) chocolate fragrance oil (optional)

I used unsweetened baking chocolate as one of the primary fats in the soap calculation. I didn't use any fragrance or added color.

The mixture produced more fumes than most, about the same as milk soap. In the Milk Chocolate Variation (below), I used Cool Technique, and the fumes were then much less.

The soap traced fairly quickly, though not accelerated. It set very quickly. A light dusting of cocoa solids rose to the top of the molds as the soap set. If desired, this could be removed in a manner similar to removing soda ash. Actually, the "frosting" is very attractive, much like the cocoa dusting on a chocolate truffle, but it's easily damaged as the soaps are unmolded.

The finished soap had a strong natural chocolate scent. The lather was brown.

I was very impressed with the way my hands felt after washing with this soap—soft and smooth. Almost like I'd used lotion.

Cocoa Butter Variation—You might substitute half the quantity of cocoa butter for the baking chocolate (4.5 ounces or 128 grams). This would make a light-colored soap, unless a discoloring fragrance oil is used.

Milk Chocolate Variation—Since milk chocolate varies so much by brand, I constructed "milk chocolate" from known ingredients. I substituted half and half (light cream) for the water and added 1½ teaspoons of sugar. Because of the cream and sugar, I used Cool Technique. The soap traced quickly. I'd hoped the cream would make it lighter-colored, like a chocolate candy bar, but it didn't. It was as dark as the Dark Chocolate Soap. Further experiments in lightening the color by replacing some of the chocolate with cocoa butter or by adding titanium dioxide would be possible.

Cocoa Butter Soap

If you use cocoa butter that hasn't been deodorized, you get a good chocolate scent. I recommend making this one in tray or individual molds. Cocoa butter, like milk products, can overheat, resulting in bull's-eye discoloration. Consider chilling molds for an hour or so after pouring.

> 7.5 ounces (213 grams) almond oil
> 9 ounces (255 grams) cocoa butter
> 13.5 ounces (383 grams) coconut oil
> 9 ounces (255 grams) water
> 4.5 ounces (128 grams) lye
> Optional: 1.2 ounces (34 grams) chocolate fragrance oil

White Chocolate Variation—Commercial white chocolate contains too much sugar and too little cocoa butter to be ideal for soapmaking. Using the same approach as with milk chocolate, I modified the cocoa butter soap recipe by using half and half (light cream) for the liquid, adding 1½ teaspoons sugar before freezing it. White chocolate fragrance oil is available, and would add to the interest of this soap.

Chocolate Coconut Soap

I must admit, I fell in love with coconut oil soap after trying it for my January entry. Here's a chocolate version.

> 30 ounces (851 grams) coconut oil
> 9 ounces (255 grams) commercial or homemade chocolate milk, frozen
> 4.4 ounces (125 grams) lye

Use Cool Technique. This soap won't have noticeable chocolate scent, unless you use a chocolate fragrance.

I made this with homemade chocolate milk (added 1 teaspoon natural cocoa and 1 teaspoon sugar to the milk and blended well before freezing). The color was darker than chocolate milk soap I've made with commercial chocolate milk.

Time to trace was unusually long, and the fumes were unusually pungent, even with the frozen liquid. Make sure you have excellent ventilation when you make this one.

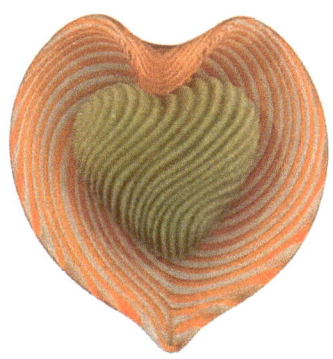

Chocolate-ish Soap

The only chocolate in this one is the fragrance. Expect fairly quick trace.

This is a "leftovers" soap. You can combine whatever oils you have in the cupboard, even if there's not much, to make fine soap. Just check the lather and other values on SoapCalc to make sure you'll like it.

- 1.5 ounces (43 grams) castor oil
- 9 ounces (255 grams) grapeseed oil
- 1.5 ounces (43 grams) refined wheat germ oil
- 3 ounces (85 grams) hemp butter
- 9 ounces (255 grams) coconut oil
- 3 ounces (85 grams) avocado butter
- 2 ounces (57 grams) chocolate fragrance, or as recommended by vendor
- 9 ounces (255 grams) water
- 4.1 ounces (118 grams) lye

The "dark chocolate" fragrance oil I used in this soap did have a rich chocolate scent in the bottle. However, the finished soap did not actually smell much like chocolate, compared to the real thing. In fact, the vanilla character of the fragrance came through more strongly than the chocolate. Different vendors' fragrances will vary, but this one was far from impressive as a chocolate scent.

Chocolate Scents

Chocolate essential oils and absolutes are available but expensive. They do survive saponification to a degree but may fade. This is one scent I'd definitely add at trace, to minimize the effect of the lye.

Most soapmaking vendors sell only chocolate fragrance oils, rather than the natural product. These fragrances may be a pure chocolate scent, or may be mixed with mint, coffee, almond, or other fragrances. All the ones I checked were discoloring fragrances—they turned the soap brown. That's an advantage in the case of chocolate soap—unless it also makes brown lather. If you're not sure, ask the vendor what to expect.

But just as with natural chocolate color, the lather will probably be dark if the soap is dark.

Vanilla and Discoloring

Fragrances that contain vanilla—as chocolate fragrances often do—will discolor cold process soap to various shades of tan or brown, depending on how much vanilla is in the fragrance. And many more fragrances contain vanilla than you might think at first.

Food scents are very likely to contain it—even some of the fruit fragrances. Rich, spicy fragrances like frankincense or dragon's blood may also contain enough vanilla to discolor. You have to rely on your vendor for this information. It should be posted with the fragrance information, but if it isn't, ask.

Vanilla stabilizer exists, but it's only recommended for melt and pour soap. It may work temporarily in cold process soap.

The color change happens from the outside in. If you were to cut a bar of soap in half a few days after pouring it into the mold, it wouldn't have turned brown in the middle. It would look like a chocolate-covered candy. Eventually, the whole soap will discolor.

A non-discoloring vanilla fragrance is available, but most soapmakers agree that its scent isn't as true as the best of the discoloring vanillas. None of the vanilla-containing fragrance blends seem to feature it.

What Would I Do?

If I were making soap to sell, I'd be very experimental with chocolate soaps. I've heard over and over that they just don't sell in some markets.

I'd be just as slow to market any soap that had dark lather. You may get customer complaints if the soap creates a mess in the tub or shower, or if it stains pale towels.

I'd definitely make cocoa butter soap again. It has a lovely silky texture, and the pale color would make it good for use with natural colorants.

Resizing a Soap Recipe

Do you really need to recalculate when you resize?

The standard advice for resizing a recipe is to recalculate the lye and liquid. Supposedly, the increase or decrease in the amounts of those ingredients may not be exactly a factor of the increase or decrease in the recipe. I say it myself in my books.

I have to admit, I got caught in a soapmaking myth. To some extent, anyway.

Numerous calculations have verified what some readers have told me—if you double the oils in a soap recipe, the lye and liquid amounts come out double when you recalculate. Or whatever multiple you use, whether it's doubling, halving, or multiplying by ten, the lye and liquid amounts won't increase or decrease unpredictably.

However, it's always a good idea to check a recipe. Especially if you haven't made it before, it's necessary to check. I get questions and cries for help regularly from people who've unsuspectingly made a bad recipe they got online, or even from a book.

Also, if you're a beginner, please don't rush into big batches too soon. They truly are a bit harder to handle—not seriously difficult, but not as easy as a small batch. Get a little experience under your belt first, and be careful to mix thoroughly—you can get uneven trace in a big pot of soap if you don't.

Soaps from the Past—Marseille Soap

Trade card for Lautz Bros. Marseilles White Soap

Marseille soap is "soap from the past" in one sense: It was legally defined by Louis XIV in 1688 in the Edict of Colbert. It is produced by a hot process that takes approximately two weeks, and involves large vats of salt water—originally water from the Mediterranean Sea.

In another sense, it is not "past," because it is still made. It is absolutely excellent soap. The lather is much better than the lather of any cold process 100% olive oil soap I've made or tried.

Originally restricted to 100% olive oil, Marseille soap was made fairly early in a version called "Marseille white soap," using a combination of palm and coconut oils.

The traditional shape, curiously, is a cube.

Nineteenth-century Marseille soap factory

MARCH

LAUNDRY SOAP

Castile Soap

Increasing Lather

Homemade Laundry Soap—Why?

Economy is the main reason most people make their own laundry soap—that and control of contents.

Ingredients for Homemade Laundry Soap

Recommended fats for making laundry soap are coconut oil, tallow, lard, palm oil, and palm kernel oil. The superfatting level is generally agreed to be 0%. Our skin can use the extra oils provided by superfatting. Clothes can't.

With automatic washers, another thing to think about is that lower sudsing is important. In a washing machine, excess suds can cause a problem called "suds lock." The machine has both an inner and an outer tub, and when there is too much sudsing, the two can get linked together by the suds. This puts a huge load on the motor and the drain pump. It's especially likely in a front-loading washer.

So, I'd recommend fairly low lather numbers on your formulation. You won't save any money on laundry detergent if you just mess up your washing machine.

If you're using a washboard, of course, this isn't a factor. But a high-lather laundry soap may be difficult to rinse out of your clothes.

Soapmakers have a choice of either bar soap or liquid. Either way, most begin by making a solid soap such as those in the recipes below. If a liquid is desired, the solid soap is grated and dissolved in boiling water, at the rate of approximately 1 cup of water per ounce of soap.

When the soap is dissolved, borax and washing soda are added:

1.8 ounces (51 grams) of borax per ounce of soap
2.2 ounces (60 grams) of washing soda per ounce of soap

The mixture is stirred until the borax and washing soda dissolve. This concentrate is poured into a larger container, and 1 quart of hot water per ounce of soap is added. It is then allowed to sit until it gels, at least overnight.

Stir before using. Use a quarter cup for each load in a front loading washer, twice that for a top loader.

Solid soap is simply grated and used like laundry detergent. Usually, borax and washing soda are also used in the wash load, in accordance with their manufacturer's quantity directions. Some soapmakers incorporate the borax and washing soda into the soap formulation. Some also use white vinegar in the rinse cycle to remove any soap scurf from the clothes and prevent clogging the machine.

I would use this with warm or hot water in the washing machine, not with cold.

Basic Laundry Soap #1

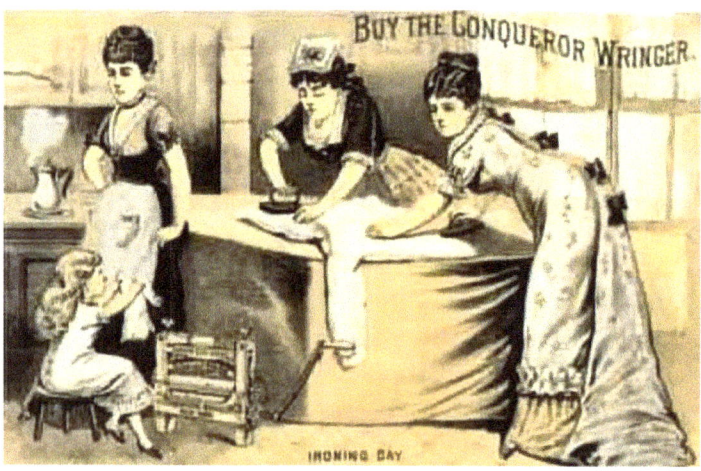

This is the typical, traditional laundry soap made by past generations—an all-lard soap with no superfatting.

    30 ounces (851 grams) lard
    9 ounces (255 grams) water
    4.2 ounces (120 grams) lye

Tallow Variation—It's possible to use beef tallow, but if you do, increase the lye to 4.2 ounces (121 grams).

Basic Laundry Soap #2

Soap Foam was powdered, supposedly making it easier to use

A vegetable-fat soap with approximately the same lather profile as lard soap. I've tested this on a washboard, but not in my washing machine.

> 25.5 ounces (723 grams) palm oil
> 4.5 ounces (128 grams) palm kernel oil flakes
> 9 ounces (255 grams) water
> 4.4 ounces (125 grans) lye

If you prefer not to use either animal products or palm products, the next best choice is probably 100% olive oil Castile. See the recipes below.

Grating Soap

How do you grate soap, anyway?

I was warned against using my coffee grinder to try to make soap powder, so I didn't.

I decided that soap has a texture similar to Parmesan cheese, so I tried two grating methods that work well for that.

On the left side of the photo are the fine shreds produced by a medium Microplane grater.

On the right side of the photo are the large granules or small lumps I got by cutting the soap into quarter-inch cubes and processing them in a food processor with the steel blade.

Both were very fast and easy to do. Either will work. The shreds will probably dissolve faster than the lumps.

And both the tools I used are about as far from the old tin graters that used to be given away with laundry soap as an iron spoon is from a stick blender.

Soaps from the Past—Laundry the Old Way

Alleged progress abounds in ironies. Why didn't they invent tumble-dry fabrics before they invented the voluminous petticoats women used to wear? But no, it was the other way around. And the more magic fabrics and dryers we have, the fewer clothes we wear . . .

—Peg Bracken, *A Window over the Sink*

Both sides of a Victorian trade card for Pearline Washing Compound

It has been said that laundry machines cause more problems than they solve, by increasing standards of cleanliness to the point where no labor is saved. This claim is beyond ridiculous.

Nineteenth- and early twentieth-century laundry methods were incredibly laborious. First, soap had to be made—and this may actually have involved rendering the fats and making lye from wood ashes. Then the soap was grated, the clothes washed on a washboard in a boiler, rinsed, hung on a line to dry, starched, and ironed with "sad irons," which were heated without electricity. I'd like to see anyone who would trade their washer/dryer and permanent press for that.

It was grueling work, involving bending, scrubbing, and hauling large tubs of very hot water. Women and servants were the designated launderers, and men might be regarded as henpecked or effeminate if they helped, even if the woman was pregnant.

Nineteenth-century washboard. Some were wood like this one, many were metal. Washboards for delicate items were made of glass.

The women who used this "sad iron" would have been surprised to know it's now a decorative collectible. "Sad" in this case means heavy, though I doubt anyone felt much joy in ironing with these things, either. They were heated in a stove or fireplace and got some of their ironing power from sheer weight. The wood handle is detachable.

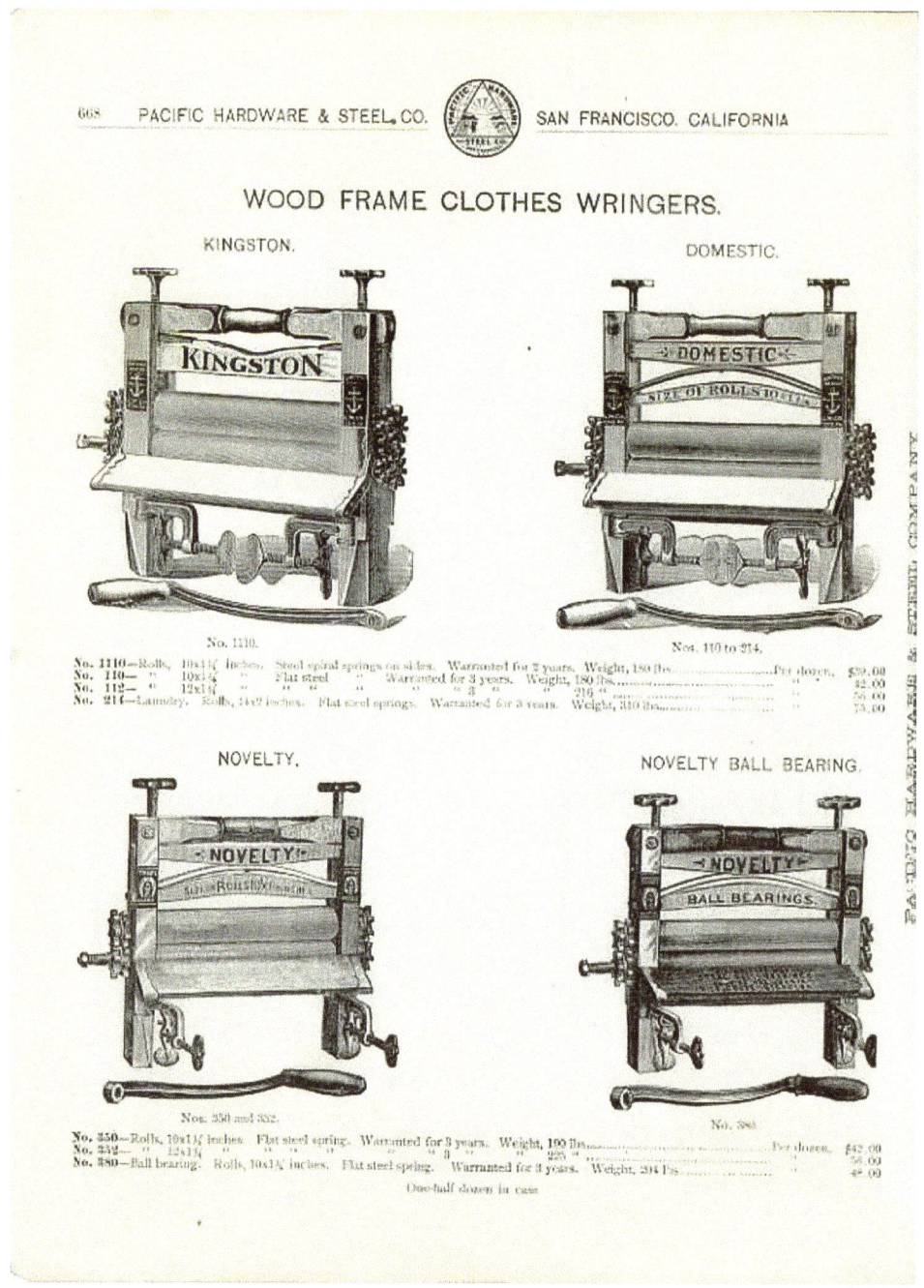

Various clothes wringers, from Pacific Hardware and Steel Company's 1902 catalog.

As time went on, some acknowledgement of the misery of current laundry methods crept into advertising. Purchased laundry soaps became available, at first advertised as economical, then, more and more, as labor saving. They were made in flakes or powder, saving the labor of grating. Various ingredients were touted as making the process easier.

Advertising showed well-dressed women, completely unruffled, using the product. Or little girls were pictured, happily laundering doll clothes.

Probably, none of these products was much of an improvement on the others.

Very few soapmakers today, if any, would wish to go back to those days. What they want is an economical, practical product they can use in an automatic washer.

MARCH

The trade cards above tout the ease of different products. It's fairly safe to guess that none of them lived up to the advertising, as far as effortlessness is concerned. If any product could have made washboard laundry into child's play, there would have been no need for the automatic washing machine to be invented.

Castile Soap—Why?

Castile is a gentle soap that's perfect for many uses, including bathing, laundry, even washing pets—assuming you avoid adding any contents that aren't good for them! (Not all handcrafted dog soap recipes do avoid that.)

Castile Soap Experiments

I've made excellent Castile soap with the cold process method. I've also made some that fell far short of what I wanted. Most of the soapmakers I know will say the same when the subject comes up.

100% olive oil soaps present some special problems for the soapmaker. One problem is long time-to-trace. Another is long curing time. A third is scanty, slimy lather. A fourth, possibly related to curing time, is inadequate hardness.

When I decided to "crack the code," I began by buying commercial olive oil soaps as well as handcrafted examples. I wanted to get some idea what I was aiming at. They varied, but at the very least, they all had good lather. Some had denser, more creamy lather than others, but none of them were slimy.

Researching early soaps, I learned that all-vegetable oil soaps developed as luxury soaps, and as far as the record goes, they were made in factories. The manufacturing processes were hot processes, involving prolonged boiling. Marseille soap, also an olive oil product, took about two weeks to make, and it was made with seawater.

This got me thinking. What if I used HP or CPOP for Castile soap? And what if I used salt water? Some sources claim this helps cut the sliminess that plagues Castile lather.

I did more research on what other soapmakers are doing and found those recommendations, along with other ideas.

• Use 5% castor oil to help with trace and lather.
• Use 1 teaspoon of sugar per pound of oils to help with trace and lather.
• Substitute KOH for 5% of the NaOH. (Courtesy of Curious Soapmaker.)
• Add a small amount of finished soap to help emulsify the lye and oils. (Also from Curious Soapmaker.)
• In my experience, some stick blenders handle olive oil soaps better than others.

Another idea that occurred to me was that most of my CP soaps contain some hard fats, which I melt and mix with the liquid fats. This means that the entire fat mixture is somewhat warm when I add the lye solution. But I've always made olive oil soaps with room temperature oil. What if I warmed the olive oil slightly to help speed trace?

The recommended amount of salt to add to soap was a half teaspoon per pound of oils, so I decided to try that. And, since hot process is something I haven't explored much, I decided to try CPOP, at least at first.

This gave me a handful of ideas to start with. I tried them in various batches of soap.

They apparently all work. Or possibly, the good results were mostly a product of the hot processing, and the other changes may or may not have helped much. Adding sugar and/or castor oil did make the lather thicker and more stable.

As always, I haven't tested every possibility on a structured, scientific basis. I encourage others to pursue my ideas as well as their own, and contact me if they want to follow up.

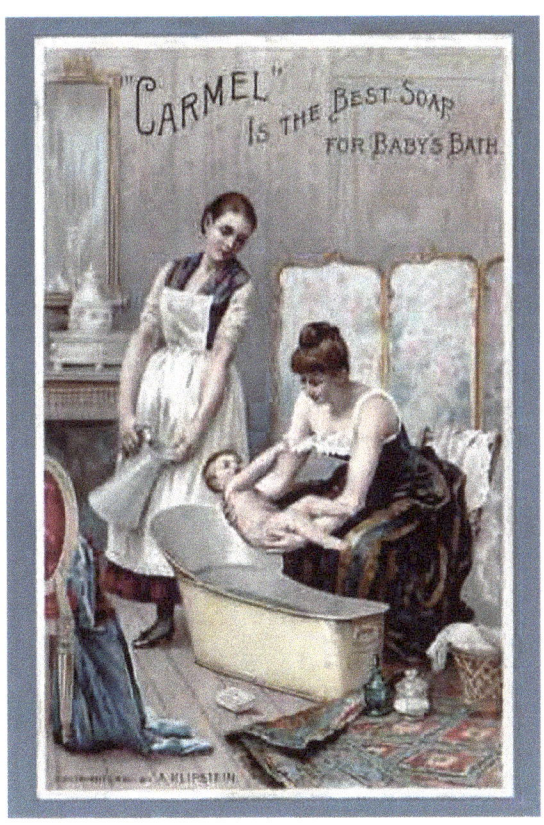

Castile baby soap advertisement

Easy Castile Soap with Variations

Make this in a two-pound log mold. You need a good stick blender for this to really count as "easy." The sugar and salt improve the lather and probably reduce the curing time.

    30 ounces (851 grams) olive oil
    9 ounces (255 grams) water
    1 teaspoon non-iodized salt, optional
    2 teaspoons sugar, optional
    3.8 ounces (109 grams) lye (sodium hydroxide)

1. Preheat oven to 150°F (65°C).
2. Dissolve sugar and/or salt in water. Dissolve lye in water.
3. Heat olive oil to about 110°F (43°C).
4. Add lye to olive oil and blend to trace.
5. Pour into mold, cover, and oven process for two hours. Turn off heat and leave mold in oven until it comes to room temperature.
6. Unmold and slice soap.
7. Let the soap cure for at least two weeks.

Castor Oil Variation

Use 28.5 ounces (808 grams) of olive oil and 1.5 ounces (43 grams) of castor oil. Lye and water amounts are unchanged. Salt and/or sugar are optional.

This variation may take longer to set and harden. It's not a "purist's Castile" according to modern soapmaking standards, although soaps labeled as Castile contained vegetable oils other than olive from a rather early date. This variation produces more bubbly lather than pure olive oil soap would probably have.

KOH Variation

For the 3.8 ounces (109 grams) of sodium hydroxide, substitute 3.7 ounces (104 grams) of sodium hydroxide and .3 ounces (8.4 grams) of potassium hydroxide. Sugar and/or salt may be used. CPOP as above. The soap will be much softer when the CPOP process is complete, but will harden as it cools.

I thought this was the most successful of my Castile soaps, although they were all good. This version lathers better than soap made with all NaOH, because KOH produces a more soluble soap—which is why it's used for liquid soap.

Grated Soap Variation

I added .18 ounces (5 grams) of finely grated Castile soap to the water, and stirred gently until it was dissolved. Then added the lye and proceeded per the recipe, except I didn't heat the olive oil, since I wanted to see if the grated soap would make the soap trace faster by itself.

The grated soap speeded up trace—a lot. But there was a disadvantage. The lye solution was opaque and contained granules. I stirred long enough to be satisfied that the granules were soap, not lye. But this is one soap that should be tested thoroughly with pH papers after oven processing, to make sure it doesn't have specks of lye in it.

When I first sliced the loaf, I could see traces of the grated soap, but they disappeared as the soap cured.

Laundry Soap Variation

For laundry soap, you want 0% superfatting, so increase the lye to 4.1 ounces (115 grams). Don't use sugar, salt, or castor oil.

Dog Soap Variation

The recipe is superfatted at 5%. If your dog's skin is dry, increase the superfatting. You can increase to as high as 8%.

Increasing Lather

Everyone likes good lather, in Castile soap or in any other. In addition to the castor oil and KOH variations discussed above for Castile, here are some ways to increase it.

Lather Boosting Ingredients

Oils—The commonly used soapmaking fats that boost bubbly lather are coconut, fractionated coconut, palm kernel, babassu, and castor. Creamy lather is increased by many fats, including castor, cocoa butter, most animal fats, olive oil, and wheat germ oil. For a complete table of soapmaking fats and their qualities, visit the SoapCalc web site.

Liquids—Liquids that contain sugars or carbohydrates increase bubbly lather. Some seem to work better than others. Beer is excellent. Milk products are also very helpful. Fruit juices can be helpful. Most of these liquids should be used frozen to prevent the lye from burning the sugars.

Additives—Sugar and similar products such as honey can be used in small amounts to boost bubbly lather. Dissolve in the water or other liquid and freeze.

Ingredients to Consider Avoiding

Some ingredients are said to decrease lather, although not everyone agrees about this.

Stearic Acid—May increase creamy lather but decrease bubbly.

Beeswax—If more than about 2% of the oils, it may decrease lather.

Titanium Dioxide—Sometimes said to decrease lather. Other soapmakers say it does not.

Surface Texture

A bar of soap with a ridged surface has more surface area than a flat one. This produces better lather. As the soap is used, the surface texture lasts longer than I would have expected.

Some single bar molds have strong patterns or ridges on the surface. A block of soap can be cut with a crinkle cutter.

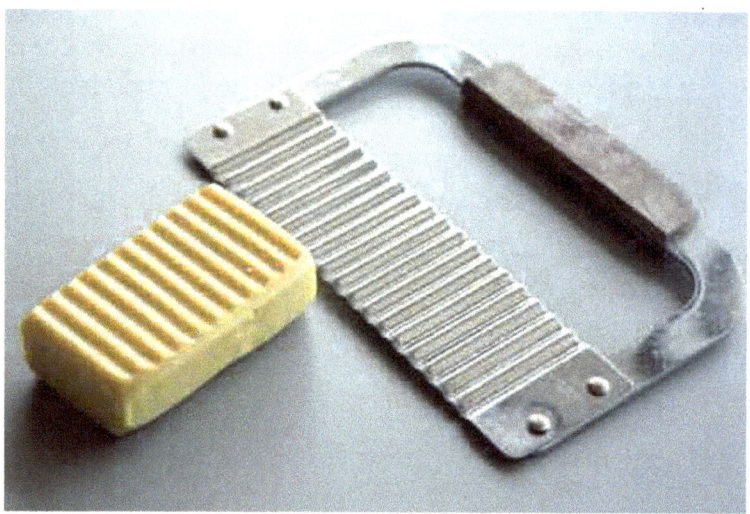

Crinkle cutter with bar of Castile soap. The ridges improve the lather quite a bit.

Accessories

A net or mesh bag will increase lather, because it grates the soap. The best net bags I ever used were made of a fine tulle called English netting. Acrylic or nylon soap saver pouches or sisal bags will also help a soap lather.

Water

Hard water produces poor lather. If you live in an area with hard water, you may get a major improvement by using water softener.

Soap lathers better in warm water than in cold.

Dog Soap

Castile soap is gentle, and probably the best choice for dog soap.

Reading articles about handcrafted dog soap, I was puzzled to see that so many recommend the use of essential oils that are also commonly used as dog *repellents*. I asked my veterinarian about this. Her opinion is that no scent of any kind should be used in a dog soap. Dogs' sense of smell is keener than ours, and many of them are distressed by strong odors that aren't natural to a dog.

She also said that their skin is delicate, and different from ours. The pH of a dog's skin is less acidic than human skin. Individual dogs may have either dry or oily skin. They may also have allergies, fleas, and irritation from licking.

If you make soap for your dog, pay attention to the way the dog responds to it. If it seems to cause irritation or dryness, use higher superfatting in the next batch. The pH for dog soap should be 7 or slightly below.

If a dog has fleas, I believe it's best to consult your veterinarian, rather than try to formulate a home treatment.

What Would I Do?

So, what would I do if I were making Castile soap for myself?
I'd use the KOH variation with the added salt and sugar.
I'd warm the olive oil before mixing with the other ingredients.

I wouldn't go any farther out of my way to improve time to trace, because my stick blender makes short work of olive oil soap in any case. (But if anyone else tries liquid soap to accelerate trace, I'd love to hear about it!)

I'd CPOP the soap, slice it with a crinkle cutter, and remember to use it in warm water.

When you CPOP soap, remember to keep the windows open. Your oven probably vents into your house, and depending on your sensitivity to fumes, you may be creating an irritating atmosphere.

Soaps from the Past—Historical Castile Soap

Unlike Marseille soap, Castile was not defined and limited by law. Traditionally made only of vegetable fats, Castile was not limited to olive oil, or to any particular oil. As early as the late nineteenth century, advertising trade cards describe "Castile" soap made of other oils. This was described as an advantage, so there must not have been any particular feeling that Castile soap "should" be an olive oil soap, although it almost certainly was originally that.

Because the term has been stretched to cover so many mild soaps with vegetable fat bases, it's very difficult to research the development of Castile as an olive oil soap.

The nineteenth-century advertisement below shows that "Castile" could mean any vegetable oil soap. The advertised product, made from cottonseed oil, was probably not very similar to the olive oil Castile soaps of Europe. It's interesting that this soap is also advertised as a floating soap, and there were others at that time, as well. It came as news to me that Ivory was not the first floating soap.

APRIL

EGG SOAPS

Designing Soaps for Different Uses
Analyzing and Fixing Problems

Eggs in Soapmaking—Why?

In answering this, we have to keep in mind that egg yolks and egg whites have completely different properties and are used differently in soapmaking.

Egg Yolks

Yolks are treated as another fat in soapmaking. They produce a rich, thick lather. An egg yolk contains about five grams of fat. Mix with the liquid fats before adding the melted solid fats.

Here are the fatty acids in egg yolk with their typical percentages, according to the US National Research Council. The properties of those fats for soapmaking are from SoapCalc.

Oleic acid
Bubbly lather, creamy lather, conditioning
47%

Palmitic acid
Hardness, creamy lather
23%

Linoleic acid
Conditioning
16%

Palmitoleic acid
Bubbly lather, creamy lather, conditioning
5%

Stearic acid
Hardness, creamy lather
4%

Linolenic acid
Conditioning
2%

Myristic acid
Hardness, cleansing, bubbly lather
1%

Egg Whites

The whites contain no fat. The protein in egg white has an astringent effect on the skin. Commercial egg white soaps are made with rose water, which may add to that effect.

Egg Yolk Soap

This soap had thick, rich lather, with no eggy smell.

> 12 ounces (340 grams) palm kernel flakes
> 15 ounces (425 grams) olive oil
> 1.5 ounces (43 grams) castor oil
> 1.5 ounces (43 grams) refined wheat germ oil
> 2 egg yolks
> 9 ounces (255 grams) water
> 4.3 ounces (122 grams) lye

1. Melt the palm kernel flakes.
2. Combine the liquid fats with the egg yolks, blend thoroughly.
3. Slowly blend in the melted palm kernel oil.
4. Add lye solution and blend to trace.

Swedish Egg White Soap

I didn't have a recipe for traditional Swedish egg white soap, if there is such a thing. What I did have was a small bar that was called that, and I noticed several things about the ingredients list on the box it was packaged in. One was that the soap was made, at least partly, with rosewater. The other was that there was not a lot of egg white in it.

So, I formulated a recipe with all this in mind.

> 3 ounces (8 grams) rosewater
> 1 teaspoon dehydrated egg white
> 4.5 ounces (128 grams) palm kernel oil flakes
> 3 ounces (85 grams) shea butter
> 10.5 ounces (298 grams) coconut oil
> 9 ounces (255 grams) olive oil
> 3 ounces (85 grams) refined wheat germ oil
> 9 ounces (255 grams) water
> 4.4 ounces (126 grams) lye

1. Combine the rosewater and egg white. Blend thoroughly. Set aside.
2. Dissolve lye in water.
3. Melt the solid fats, add to the liquid fats.
4. Add the lye solution and blend to light trace. Add the rosewater mixture and continue blending. It will be stringy at first, but will smooth out.

My purchased egg white soap was pale pink and smelled strongly of roses. I believe it would be necessary to use a fragrance or essential oil to get this level of scent. It's possible that having the entire liquid quantity be rosewater might do it. A good natural colorant to produce a pale pink would be alkanet root. (See November.)

The soap I made from this recipe had great lather. It was not nearly as astringent as the purchased product. No eggy smell.

APRIL

Cool Whole Egg Soap

    I read quite a few complaints that egg soaps turned out to have a bad smell. While this wasn't my experience with egg yolk soap, I decided to design one recipe with whole eggs to see what happened. I used Cool Technique, so the lye would not react very much with the egg.

> 4.9 ounces (138 grams) avocado butter
> 15 ounces (425 grams) coconut oil
> 8.3 ounces (234 grams) olive oil
> 1.8 ounces (53 grams) castor oil
> 2 beaten eggs
> 9 ounces (255 grams) frozen milk or cream
> 4.5 ounces (128 grams) lye

    1. Melt the solid fats and allow to cool slightly. Add to the liquid fats. Add the eggs and blend to mix thoroughly.
    2. Dissolve the lye in the frozen milk and add to the oil mixture. Stick blend to trace.
    3. Treat as any Cool Technique milk soap. (You may want to give this one a short time in the freezer before unmolding.)
    What did I get? Excellent lather. And there was no eggy smell in the finished soap.

    Cool Egg White Soap Variation—Make this with two egg whites rather than two whole eggs. This would make a soap similar to early egg white soaps that were made with cream.

Does Egg Soap Spoil Quickly?

According to people who make and use it, the belief that egg soap spoils quickly is a myth.

The rectangles are egg white soap, the rounds are whole egg soap, and the ovals (seen side view) are egg yolk soap.

Designing Soaps for Different Uses

When we design a soap, it's good to go beyond simple chemistry. If possible, design for use. Here are desirable qualities to target for different kinds of soap.

Bath Soap

- Good hardness, since these soaps may spend more time in water than most.
- Medium cleansing and conditioning. (This would vary with the user's needs.)
- Good bubbly lather.

Hand Soap

• Good cleansing and conditioning. Need for cleansing varies, but for general-use hand soap, I'd expect medium to high values in both.
• Good bubbly lather, medium creamy lather.

Facial Soap

• Design for skin type—higher conditioning value for dry skin, higher cleansing value for oily.
• Avoid comedogenic oils, even in dry skin soaps.

Scrub Soaps

Scrub soaps may be hand soaps with some kind of abrasive in them. Abrasives vary in "scrubbiness," and it's important to choose one that's right for the job. A gardener or mechanic may want something fairly coarse, such as coffee grounds, coarse orange peel, or even sand.

An exfoliating facial soap, on the other hand, would use something gentler, like oat flour or pulverized orange or cucumber peel.

The amount of scrub will vary not only with the additive, but with how much of it is used. And to some extent, with how long the soap is in use and whether it dries out between uses. Some additives, such as minced citrus peel, may become considerably harder and scratchier as the soap ages.

Analyzing and Fixing Problems

Help! What went wrong?
I get questions from people with soap problems—fortunately, they're almost never problems with my books or recipes. But the soap gremlins can cause a lot of trouble. Here are some of the common questions, and my best troubleshooting advice.

* * *

I've made soap before with no problems, but now it suddenly has stopped working.

What changed? New ingredients, new equipment? Bigger batch? Different vendors? New technique? Isolate what is different, and most of the time, you'll put your finger on what went wrong.

I can't emphasize this enough. If you can identify what changed, you usually have the solution to the problem. This is the main thing I ask about when a previously successful reader contacts me with a failure.

Or, if it's the reader's first batch, I ask how they deviated from the directions. Years ago, a reader wrote to me to say she was annoyed that my Shea Supreme soap had not worked. And the "only" change she'd made was to add a whole banana.

* * *

My soap won't set.

Assuming you had a decent recipe to begin with—check your recipe!—and that you didn't make a measuring error, it may have cooled too fast. This is especially likely with Cool Technique soaps. Put it in a warm place, like on a heat pad set on Low for a couple of hours. That often works. Careful not to overheat—this can produce ugly textures. Works best with a block or log mold—hard to keep individual bars from overheating.

* * *

I'm using individual bar plastic molds, and the soap won't unmold.

Ask the manufacturer of the mold or check their web site. You can also run a search on "release soap plastic molds."

* * *

My soap has white stuff on it.

Where? If it's on the outside, it's probably soda ash. See November for a write-up of the soda ash problem. If it's veins on the inside, it may well be lye pockets. Test with pH paper to see if the white material has a high pH. If it does, about the only hope is to rebatch it. You might also decide to simply toss it.

* * *

My soap is set, but it has something shiny on top— oil or liquid, or something.

Test with a pH paper. If the pH paper reads very high (13 or 14), you'll have to rebatch or discard the soap. If it doesn't, wait a while. Sometimes fragrance or essential oil will appear on the top of the soap mold for a short while, then it will be absorbed.

* * *

My soap has a pH of 10 to 11, and it's not decreasing any more. What did I do wrong?

Nothing. Your soap is probably fine. pH papers are not all that accurate for soap. All they can really do is alert you to a disaster—that would be a pH of 13 or 14. They don't give you an accurate pH. If your soap's pH is reading 10 to 11, and it's pleasant to use, don't worry about it.

* * *

My soap has orange spots. What did I do wrong?

"Dreaded orange spots," or DOS, are the soapmaker's despair. There's no lack of theories about them, but as far as I know, no one has come up with anything that will guarantee you won't get them. For the latest thinking, do an online search on the term.

* * *

When I sliced my soap, it had a darker core at the center. Will it go away?

This is caused by overheating after the soap is poured. You'll almost always get this if you put soap make with fragile ingredients such as milk into a block mold. I've never known a so-called "bull's-eye" to go away.

* * *

I used milk/yogurt/vegetable juice/fruit juice/egg/whatever in my soap, and I got a rancid, burned smell.

Use Cool Technique with fragile ingredients. I go into a lot of detail about this in my book *Milk Soapmaking*, and again in my book *Cool Soapmaking*. Briefly, what you do is freeze the liquid and trickle the lye onto it. Working this cold prevents burning.

* * *

My soap has a serious problem. Can I rebatch it?

Rebatching is much easier if you know exactly what went wrong—for instance if you left out an ingredient. But rebatch soap is never top quality, in my experience. The soaps feel waxy. Bars may crack and warp. If you really want to rebatch, I suggest making soap balls.

* * *

While it's not that common for soap to have problems, there are many possible problems and questions when it does. One good approach is to put the term "soap making" into your browser, along with your problem. You're likely to get dozens of good prospects for solutions.

Soaps from the Past—Additives in Soap

I'm fascinated by soap history and soap advertising. When I began paying attention to soap ads from the nineteenth and early twentieth centuries, I noticed a lot were featuring special additives. Some of these additives were said to treat skin conditions and irritations. Others were purely cosmetic. Laundry soaps, as today, typically had additives to boost cleaning power or to deodorize.

Most of these cards date from the period 1880 to 1920. Many additives later stopped being used after being legally restricted.

Quinine and sulfur in a baby soap? According to the back of the card, it "gives relief," but they don't say from what. Diaper rash? Sulfur is very drying. Quinine must be, too—quinine soap is recommended for acne in some publications.

According to the back of this trade card, you can have white hands, smooth skin, and clear complexion by using Cornell's Benzoin Cosmetic Soap. Benzoin is used today as a fragrance stabilizer and is known to irritate sensitive skin.

This card advertises "ozone soap," probably referring to ozonated olive oil. This is an old treatment to rejuvenate skin, now coming back into fashion. I could find no objective clinical information about this product.

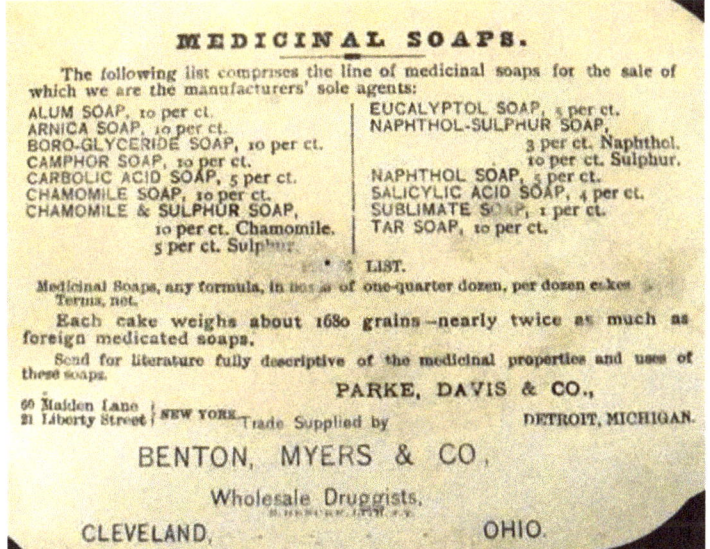

Whole menus of medicinal soaps from two specialty suppliers.

Wrapper from Lettuce Heart Soap, which was supposed to whiten skin.

Coal Oil Johnny's Petroleum Soap may have been an early detergent bar. The card mentions that the soap is transparent. Supposedly, that means it's purer—but I doubt coal oil soap would be popular today anyway.

Front and back sides of a trade card for borax soap. The poem is fun! And who could resist those kittens? Clearly, this soap was for laundry.

Carbolic disinfecting soap. A mild disinfectant and deodorant, now little used except in disaster relief areas.

MAY

SILK SOAPS

Floral and Fruit Scents

Wild, Weird, and Wonderful Soap Ads

Silk in Soapmaking—Why?

Soap trade card depicting silk manufacture

We use silk in soap for the same qualities that make it attractive as a fabric. It gives a unique smooth texture to soaps, and also to lotions and other cosmetics.

Using Silk in Soapmaking

Nineteenth-century silk workers in Italy

Silk fiber or fabric for soapmaking must be 100% silk. Silk is tough, though—you can't just add silk roving to lye water and expect it to dissolve. Chop it fine and let it soak in the water for half an hour before adding the lye. Don't use too much.

If you're using fabric, use about one square inch of fabric per pound of oils in the soap. Fabric must be clean and free of sizing or other additives. Many soapmakers prefer to use undyed fabric, but others say it makes no difference. Wet the fabric down well before adding to the lye solution. It may dissolve faster if it's cut into strips.

It's less trouble to use silk products that have been adapted for soapmaking. Many soapmaking suppliers sell silk products of various kinds—silk amino acids or powder seem to be the most common. Use per vendor's directions.

Using Floral Scents

Natural floral scents may be essential oils, absolutes, or concretes—the differences have to do with how they're produced. They all tend to be expensive.

Floral fragrance oils, both single-note and blends, are numerous and varied. Some attempt to duplicate the actual scent of a particular flower. Some do this with considerable success, others are not realistic.

Some fragrance oils, such as sunflower or marigold, aim for the "idea" of a flower that actually has no scent, or no usable one.

Blending

Floral fragrances are lovely, but with no other elements in the blend, they can seem a bit flat. Here are some ideas for introducing complexity to florals.

• Floral + musk makes a richer, warmer scent.
• Floral + a "green" scent such as green tea or leafy fragrances. This is actually the way we perceive floral scents in nature, with a background leaf fragrance.
• Floral + citrus lightens the sweetness and introduces a fresh note.
• Mixed floral, or floral and herbal—such as rose + jasmine + lavender—produces a more natural effect than a single floral note.

More Considerations

It's always best to ask your vendor if a scent accelerates trace. They don't necessarily include this information in their catalogs.

Floral scents that are often said to accelerate trace include geranium essential oil, lilac fragrance oil, and peony fragrance oil. Some rose fragrance oils do, as well, and there may well be others. See August for suggestions for working with accelerants.

Some floral fragrances need to be soaped with low temperature techniques and not allowed to gel. If they overheat, the fragrance changes or disappears. Treat as you would milk soap.

MAY

Flowers-and-Silk Soap

Designed for minimum color and odor from oils. This mixture is fairly slow to trace, which should help with fragrances that accelerate trace, or with special effects such as swirling. The "silky" feel of the fiber imparts a similar effect to the soap, giving a luxurious texture.

> 9.9 ounces (281 grams) almond butter
> 10.2 ounces (289 grams) coconut oil
> 9.9 ounces (281 grams) almond oil
> 9 ounces (255 grams) water
> 1 gram silk fiber (a wad about the size of a pecan in the shell)
> 4.3 ounces (123 grams) lye
> Fragrance or essential oil amount per vendor's
>   recommendation

1. Chop the silk fiber into lengths of no more than half an inch. Finer is better. Soak in the water for 30 minutes before adding the lye. After adding it, stir until the silk is dissolved. Strain. (Or use silk amino acids or powder per vendor's directions instead of dissolving silk fiber in the lye solution)

2. Melt the almond butter and coconut oil together. Add to the almond oil.

3. Add the lye solution and blend to trace. Add fragrance. I would use about 2 ounces (57 grams) of most scents for this quantity of oils.

This soap is slow to trace. You may want to turn this to your advantage—for example, it may be a good choice for swirls or other special effects. Or you may want to speed trace by using some of the suggestions I mention for Castile soap in March.

This recipe and the Floral Soap with Coconut Milk that follows are nearly pure white, odorless soaps. The recipes are intended to give a palette for your ideas—natural colors, scents, swirling, botanicals—whatever sparks your creativity.

Floral Soap with Coconut Milk

This is a milk soap with no dairy product to compete with the floral scent. What little scent coconut milk naturally has is destroyed in saponification. Use Cool Technique for this one. Make sure your shea butter is refined, so there's no oil scent, either.

> 9 ounces (255 grams) coconut oil
> 18 ounces (510 grams) sunflower oil
> 3 ounces (85 grams) refined shea butter
> 9 ounces (255 grams) coconut milk
> 4.2 ounces (120 grams) lye
> Fragrance or essential oil per vendor's recommendation

Using Fruit Fragrances

Fruit scents make lovely soaps for summer markets, but experiment carefully. Fruit fragrance oils may resemble hard candy more than fresh fruit.

Fruit fragrances are also plagued by discoloration, ricing, and acceleration.

Read reviews if vendors publish them. Also try the Soap Scent Review Board.

Blending

To blend fruit fragrances, for a start, think like a cook. Taste is mostly scent anyway, so if a combination of raspberry and orange appeals to you on a plate, you might also like it in a soap. Here are some possible combinations.

- multiple fruits
- fruit + floral
- fruit + spice
- fruit + vanilla
- fruit + herb
- fruit + chocolate

Either of the floral fragrance recipes given earlier would also be ideal for fruit fragrances, since both soaps are almost completely colorless and odorless before color and scent are added by the soapmaker.

Strained apple juice would make a good liquid for fruit-scented soaps. Use it frozen to prevent overheating of the fruit sugar. The juice will increase bubbly lather.

Don't use undiluted frozen juice concentrate—it's too sugary. The lye solution will overheat.

Soaps from the Past—
Wild, Weird, and Wonderful Soap Ads

In the US, commercial soapmaking accelerated around the same time that advertising exploded. The result was more than a little interesting.

Early advertising emphasized hygiene and ease of use. Some of the hygiene claims seem wildly exaggerated, even fraudulent, until you remember that soap was about all people had for fighting disease organisms before antibiotics. Lifebuoy Soap's claim to save lives was probably about 90% hopefulness and wishful thinking—but the remaining 10% mattered a lot.

On the other hand, some claims were misleading and even dangerous. Soaps promised to keep away colds, or to prevent much more serious diseases. Advertisements of this kind resulted in the development of strict standards about health claims for soaps and cosmetics.

As science and medicine led to more effective disease control—and as regulations got tougher—soap advertising began to instead emphasize beauty and success. According to the ads, the soaps made it possible for women to find husbands and for men to find jobs. Failure to use a certain brand would result in body odor, rejection by friends and loved ones, and economic disaster, according to these ads.

Here again, soap was almost the only thing available for the purpose. Air conditioning was a thing of the future for most of this period. Clothes were concealing and restrictive. Underarm deodorants hadn't been invented—or weren't especially effective. But ads promoted various brands by suggesting that one or another kind of soap could make a major difference—a doubtful idea, when carried that far. Claims of this type wound up raising standards of personal and household cleanliness, building up expectations that then needed to be met.

A whole book could be written—at least one has, in fact—on this "stick and carrot" approach to selling soap. It's bare knuckles advertising, propaganda at its best (or worst). I think we, as soapmakers, need to keep this history in mind—especially when we're tempted to question the labeling laws it inspired.

Of course, not all soap advertising involved misrepresentation. Some of it was quite fun, like Sapolio's Spotless Town, with its amusing characters and little poems. Or the goofy jingles on the back of trade cards for Wrisley's White Borax Soap. You have to admire the humor and ingenuity of the people who produced them.

One of my favorite literary scenes occurs in Jack Finney's novel, *Time and Again*, which opens with a mid-twentieth-century commercial artist working on a soap advertisement. His boredom, disgust, and sense of wasting his life propel him to accept an offer to time travel to 1882. In the end, he decides to stay there. I wonder if he ended up working on soap ads in that period as well. Maybe he was the inventor of Spotless Town—you never know.

A note about dates I've given for the following soap ads: Some are exact— particularly dates of magazine and newspaper ads. Some are based on vendor claims of the age of paper ephemera. Some are based on research about the manufacturer. If all else failed, hints like dress and hair styles, popular typeface styles, and such contributed to an educated guess.

The Wild and the Weird

1870—Buchan's Carbolic Toilet Soap would probably have been similar to Lifebuoy, which also contained carbolic acid as its active ingredient. The fine print in the top right corner claims that it "cures all eruptions" (of the skin, presumably, not volcanic eruptions).

In days before regulation of claims, such statements were common. Carbolic soap is mildly disinfectant and may well be helpful with some irritations and minor infections, but it most definitely won't affect skin cancer.

* * *

1880—Soap for All Nations—not a modest claim, but at least not harmful. It does reflect a certain narrow zeal, but the improbability of carrying it out most likely made it relatively harmless.

* * *

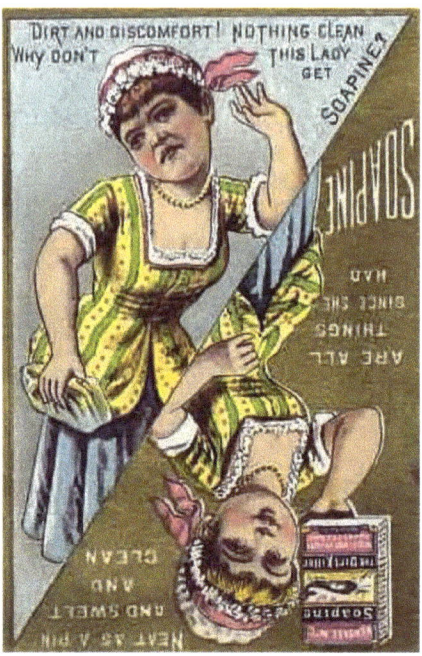

1880—An early version of the before-and-after ad.

"Dirt and discomfort! Nothing clean!
Why don't this lady get Soapine?

"Neat as a pin and sweet and clean
are all things since she had Soapine!"

Soapine was a whale blubber product that claimed not to be soap, to in fact be "better than soap." Most likely, it was soap. The whale was featured in all their early ads.

* * *

1885—Lyons Sulfur Borax Soap "prevents the contraction of contagious diseases: DIPHTHERIA, TYPHOID, and all MALARIAL FEVERS."
Diphtheria is spread through the air, typhoid by contaminated water. Malaria is transmitted by certain mosquitoes.
How in the world could a laundry soap affect that?

* * *

MAY

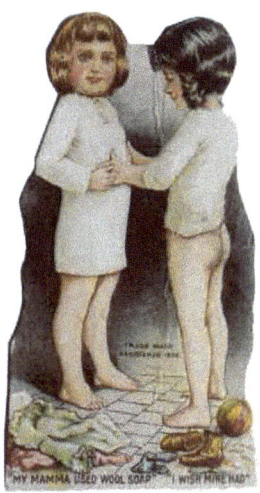

1885—"My mamma used Wool Soap!"

"I wish mine had!"

This ad for Wool Soap by Swift and Company suggests that shrinkage in wool is caused by choice of soap. Actually, the most important factor is water temperature. It's also unlikely that a shirt would shrink this much in one washing.

And then there's the implied hook—that the "good mother" uses the product, while the competitor's customer is a "bad mother" who not only ruins the shirt but leaves her child half nude.

* * *

1886—A nice poetic ad. I doubt if anyone really believed that Oakley's Queen soap would make them glad their vacation was over, but it's a nice thought.

There's a difference between painting a lovely picture and telling a downright lie—some ads manage to stay on the right side of that line. This one seems charming and quite harmless, even if it isn't exactly realistic.

***

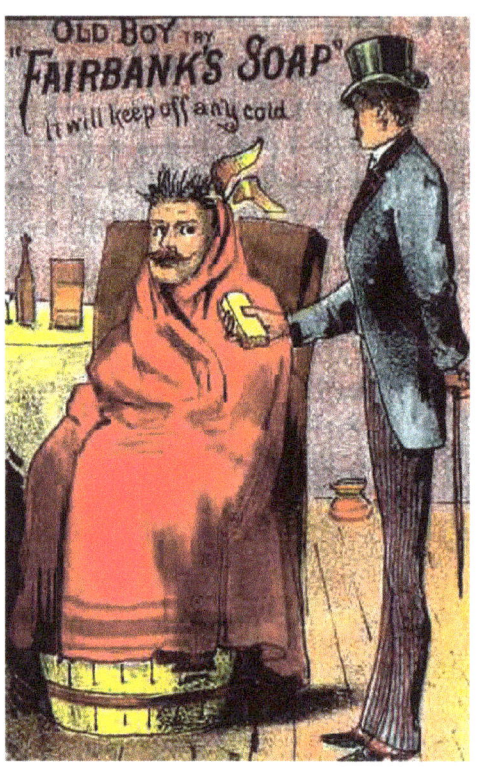

1890—Here we have Fairbank's Soap, that "will keep off any cold," though the ad doesn't say how. Hand washing is useful for helping to prevent contagion, but it won't help once a person is sick.

***

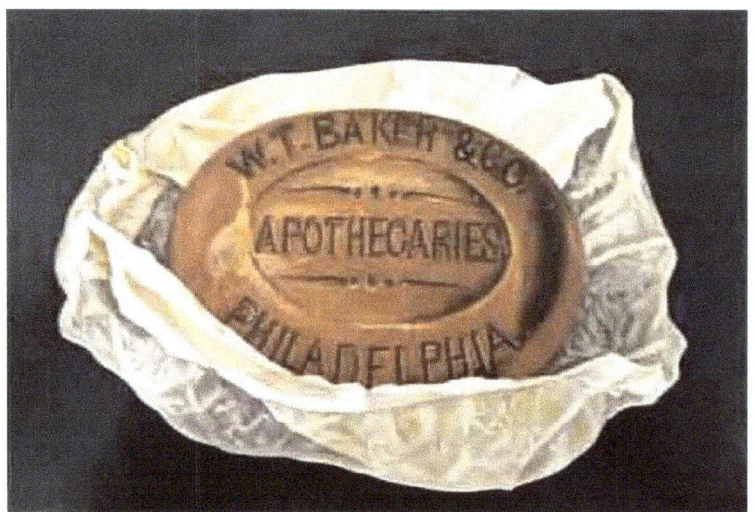

1890—This trade card interested me because it was the earliest I've seen where the illustration was actually a picture of the soap itself. The card is probably late nineteenth-century, but it has a surprisingly modern look. The reverse side of the card lists the company's medicated soaps, but makes no claims for any of them.

***

MAY

1890—Many advertisements of the late nineteenth century used games, puzzles, toys, and amusing images to sell.

Some were educational—cards that could be collected, showing birds, presidents, scenes of many lands, trades and professions, or similar picture series.

Some had coupons and special offers, premiums and giveaways. The Larkin Company, manufacturer of Sweet Home Soap, used personal testimonials on the reverse of their trade cards, as well as premiums, buying clubs, and door-to-door sales.

Several companies vied for customers by offering paper dolls and play furniture—a hint that perhaps Victorian children were not quite so "unseen and unheard" as we may have thought.

* * *

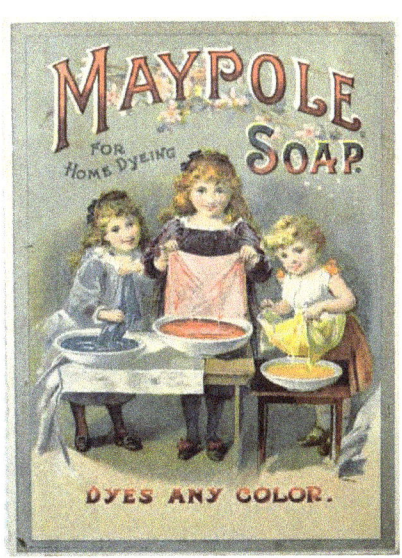

1898—Maypole wasn't the only "soap dye." It probably did help refresh color, but that wasn't the extent of its claims. The back of this card says that Maypole Soap will dye any color, even black, without boiling. Any fiber, too—although at the time this soap was made, only natural fibers were available. According to the ad, results were of professional quality.

Having given home dyeing a try myself with the old Rit dyes, I doubt this. I suspect there are good reasons why dye soap no longer exists.

***

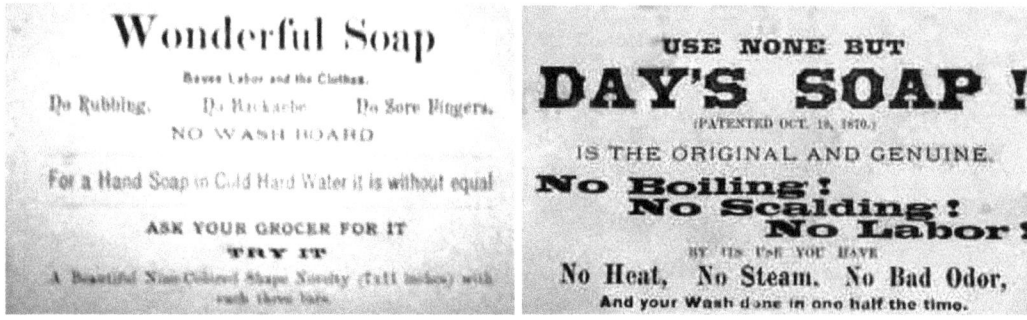

1900—Claims from two competing brands of laundry soap.
"No Rubbing . . . No Backache . . . No Sore Fingers . . . NO WASH BOARD"
"No Boiling! No Scalding! No Labor! And your Wash done in one half the time."
You have to wonder if the laundry just rose up and did itself!

***

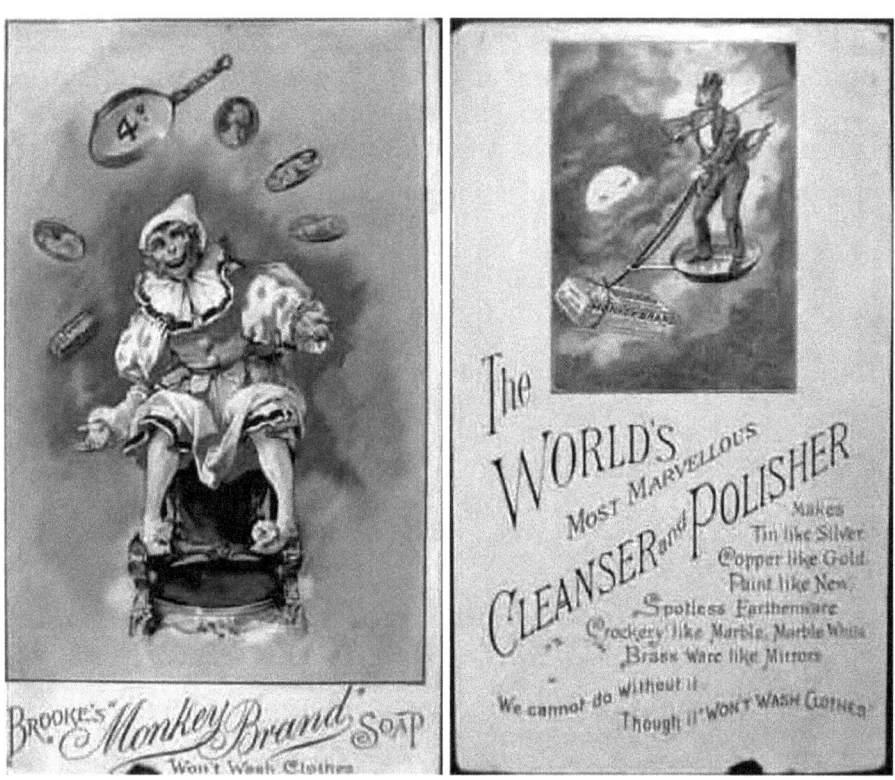

1900—Monkey Brand Soap, which must have been an abrasive soap rather like Lava, claims to make "Tin like Silver, Copper like Gold, Paint like New, Crockery like Marble, Brass ware like Mirrors."

Whether anyone believed this beyond the purchase of more than one bar of soap, it's hard to say. But claims like this and the claims that were made for patent medicines about the same time (1880–1900) are a major reason why we have the labeling requirements we have today.

***

MAY

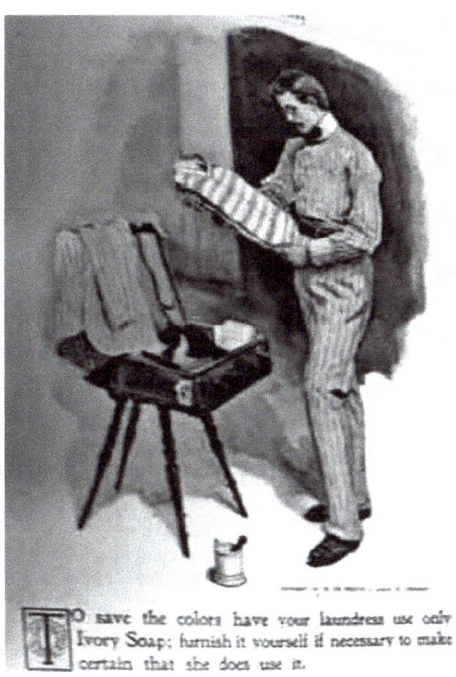

To save the colors have your laundress use only Ivory Soap; furnish it yourself if necessary to make certain that she does use it.

1901—"Have your laundress use only Ivory Soap. Furnish it yourself if necessary to make certain that she does use it."

Servants of all kinds, including laundresses, were more common when this ad appeared. But its appeal to class-consciousness is fairly open. It may have sold more soap to people who liked the idea behind the ad than to those who actually had a personal laundress.

* * *

This Photograph of Mary Priscilla Blocher, who was born Aug. 11th, 1899, was taken July 11th, 1900, when she was just eleven months old. Her parents and friends are justly proud of her beautiful, glossy and lustrous, wavy hair, and they attribute a generous share of credit, which is undoubtedly due, to the exclusive use of **Resinol Soap**, the only soap used in her daily bath since the day of her birth.

ALL DRUGGISTS SELL THIS SOAP.

Resinol Chemical Co.,
SOLE PROPRIETORS.
Baltimore, Md.,
U. S. A.

1905—So, what have we here? The text claims that the child is eleven months old, and that her beautiful hair is a result of being washed with Resinol Soap.

Wig? Maybe.

Retouched photo? Possibly.

Older child? Probably. She looks more like eighteen months old than eleven.

Some kind of thickening treatment on the hair?

Unusual baby, illogical assumptions about the soap?

Resinol is still manufactured today and is not recommended for use on children under two years old except with a doctor's advice.

It also has nothing to do with luxuriant tresses. It's a soothing ingredient, recommended for chapped skin, poison ivy, and such. If it could stimulate hair growth, there would be no more male pattern baldness.

* * *

1910—An early floating soap. The text on the reverse side of this card makes many vague claims that this product is "the best," but none are exactly spelled out. The artwork is a good example of the subconscious thrust of advertising. The woman is attractive, young, and obviously well-off, judging by her clothing and furniture.

More than soap is being sold here, but soap is actually all you can buy. This is very common in advertising. We see it also in the mid-twentieth-century use of movie and sports stars in soap advertising. If such glamorous and successful people use a particular brand of soap, some of the glamor and success rubs off on the soap itself. There's no blatant claim that I'd become famous if I used the product, but I'm encouraged to think I might become more like one of these super-people if I did.

And of course, it doesn't happen.

* * *

1914—"A woman's looks count for so much more than a man's in the sum of life that she owes it to herself to do all that she reasonably can to preserve, and if possible enhance, whatever grace and charm of person nature may have endowed her with."

For the next several decades, variations on this theme of soap = beauty = female success will turn up in different forms, time and time again.

* * *

1925—No subtlety here . . . this one is outright fraud.

***

1928—Here's a response to women entering the business work force in larger numbers. Use Palmolive soap, because that complexion is worth money, honey.

***

1929—The 1920s began a trend that was to continue for several decades—featuring movie stars in soap ads. This full-page ad featured Clara Bow. She was a major star, appearing in 46 silent films and 11 talkies.

Whether she actually used Lux soap is another matter.

MAY

* * *

1939—"This is for always, Darling!"

"Nan hopes so, too! That's why she guards against dry, lifeless, 'middle-age' skin!"

So, if her marriage fails, it will be her own fault for not using Palmolive soap?

This is blatant fear-selling. It plays to the desire for love, and to insecurity about losing it. And to magical thinking that a soap ingredient could be the fountain of youth. If olive oil soap could guarantee perpetual beauty, undying love, and a happy life, the world would be a much simpler place.

* * *

1942—Shame-selling at its best. If you don't use the product, your *underwear* will tell on you!

* * *

1942—Brides are one of the most common images in mid-twentieth-century soap advertisements. The white dresses project an image of cleanliness—though, of course, wedding dresses aren't usually laundered. More than that, a bride at that time would have been a symbol of supreme womanly triumph, the dream realized. All due to her soap, of course.

This one is a bit different. In this little playlet, a new bride phones her mother with a dilemma—her husband isn't interested.

But Cashmere Bouquet soap flies to the rescue, with the lesson that soaps that control body odor don't have to have a mannish fragrance. Honeymoon saved!

* * *

1942—"Won't *somebody* love me?"

"Somebody very nice surely will . . . if you'll just discover the secret of bathing away body odor with one soap that will actually adorn your skin with a protective fragrance . . . a fragrance men love! It's no longer necessary to risk your daintiness with an unpleasant-smelling soap!"

Further panels in this ad for Cashmere Bouquet show a friend telling her the "secret," followed by the woman receiving an enormous diamond engagement ring from a handsome man.

That's a lot to get for the price of a bar of soap.

MAY

* * *

1943—Lux Soap: a woman's patriotic duty.

* * *

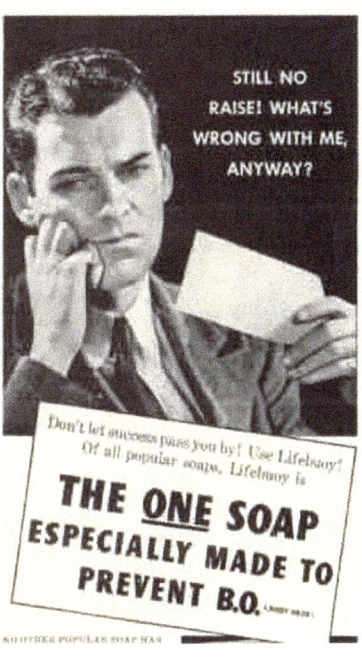

1949—"Don't let success pass you by! Use Lifebuoy!"
The undermining drumbeat wasn't confined to women. Many ads showed men being passed over for a job, raise, or promotion because they used the wrong soap.
Of course, if any one soap could deliver on the implied promises, there would be no need at all for any of the others.

* * *

1952—Here's a mid-twentieth-century ad that combines fear selling with shame selling.

"Dirt danger days" would probably be summer, when kids are likely to be outdoors. They do get grubby. This is normal, not dangerous, of course. Recent research suggests it's necessary for healthy development of the immune system.

A small justification for the idea of keeping children healthy by keeping them clean might be that, when this ad appeared, it was only the first year the polio vaccine was offered to the public. Before that, children might be suddenly struck with the disease, which seemed to be more prevalent in summer. Parents must have been very afraid of it, and must have done everything they could to make their children safe. However, it is too contagious to be prevented by soap.

The idea of dirt = danger is an effective hook for selling soap, especially when there's a bit of guilt thrown in: "If your child gets sick, it's because you, a bad parent, didn't wash him enough with our product."

* * *

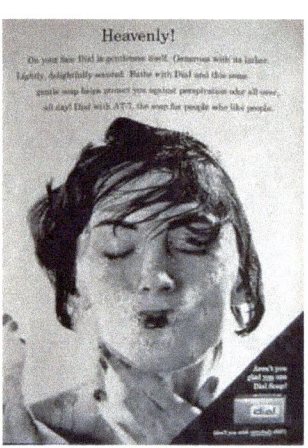

1960—"The soap for people who like people . . .

"Dial—Don't you wish everyone did?"

Another subliminal appeal to insecurity and fear. Many products were marketed this way, not just soap—mouthwash, deodorant, shampoo—anything to do with personal hygiene.

And the Wonderful

1889—Here's one ad that seems to laugh at the whole idea of advertising.

* * *

1901—And here they are—some of the residents of Spotless Town.
These fun-loving ads were famous, and they must have sold tons of soap. And they made no outrageous claims at all.

***

1901—This beautiful ad for Ivory Soap makes no special claims except that they believe you'll like it if you try it. Fair advertising at its best, from an era when outrageous claims were common.

***

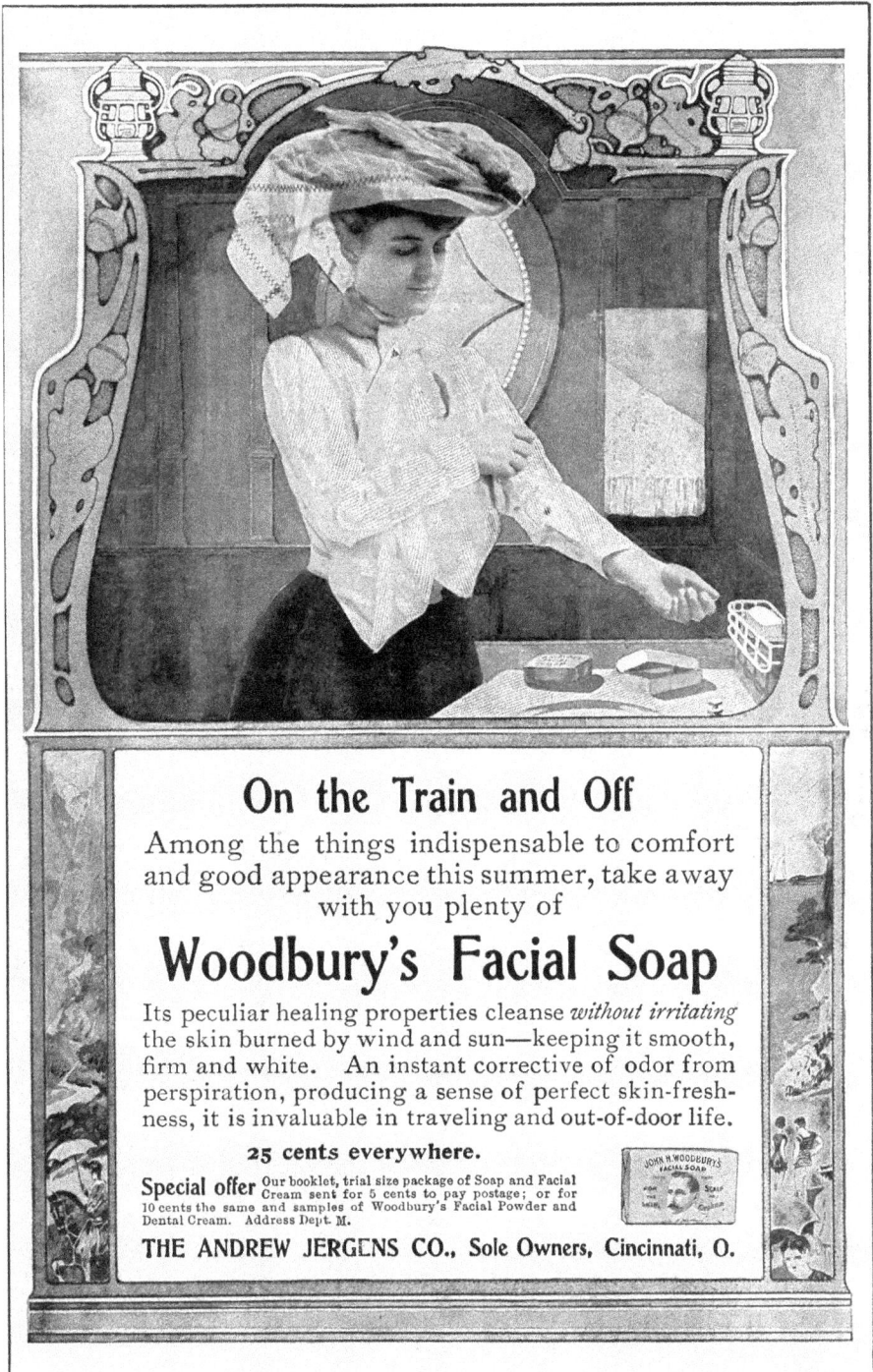

1903—And finally, an ad that promises the only thing we can claim today—that soap will get you clean.

One Last Thought

There is no link between hard-line advertising and a brand's survival. Some of the most "gentlemanly" advertisers are the companies that have lasted for over a century. And many of the less ethical ones have not stayed in business—or if they have, they've changed their tone completely. Underhanded advertising does not bring success.

JUNE
CUCUMBER SOAPS
Low Temperature Soapmaking

Cucumbers in Soapmaking—Why?

Cucumber has long been regarded as beneficial for the skin. According to the *Cambridge World History of Food*, cucumbers have been used at least since the nineteenth century in soaps and other cosmetics.

They're believed to improve the complexion, soothe the skin, and fade freckles. Cucumbers do seem to be somewhat astringent, and cool cucumber is pleasant on the skin on a hot day.

Occasionally, they're even claimed to treat more serious skin conditions. As soapmakers, we know we can't make claims of that kind. Whatever the benefits of raw cucumber, they may or may not still be present in cucumber soap.

Probably the main advantage of cucumber soap is its pleasant texture and appearance, which give it good marketability. It makes an appealing soap, especially with green flecks of cucumber peel in it.

Avoiding Burned Cucumber Odor

As I looked at recipes and comments about making cucumber soap, I stumbled across one that occurred over and over: People said the lye burns the cucumber and produces a nasty odor. Some said the odor fades, others said it doesn't. But I started wondering if it would work to treat cucumber, and possibly other fruit and vegetable soaps as well, the same way we treat milk soaps to avoid burning—freeze the liquid in ice trays, and sprinkle the lye onto the cucumber "ice cubes."

It worked perfectly. I'd strongly recommend freezing anything that's likely to burn when lye is added to it. You get better soap, with less likelihood of a "volcano." (More about that later.)

Since I was using frozen liquid anyway, I decided to try a 50-50 mixture of cucumber and yogurt in some of my soaps, in addition to making some with only cucumber juice and/or pulp as the liquid.

Basic Cucumber Soap and Variations

Since there were so many questions about how to work with cucumber, I decided to start with a basic recipe. I branched out a little after a few batches, but this basic recipe is the main one I used, given here with a few variations.

>21 ounces (595 grams) olive oil
>9 ounces (255 grams) coconut oil
>9 ounces (255 grams) frozen cucumber juice, puree, or
>   mixture of cucumber and another liquid
>4.2 ounces (121 grams) lye, bead or microbead

Cucumber Yogurt Soap

Half the liquid was frozen cucumber puree, including very finely minced peel. Half was frozen plain yogurt. I mixed the two before freezing. This formulation made a nice looking beige soap with green flecks. Lots of excellent lather, bubbly and creamy. The flecks of peel are slightly exfoliating—not as much as cornmeal or coffee grounds would be, but noticeably a little rough.

Cucumber Puree Soap

Part or all of the liquid was frozen cucumber puree. Puree in different batches was made both with and without the peel.

Olive/coconut soap with whole pureed cucumber

Cucumber Juice Soap

All the liquid was frozen cucumber juice. Juice in different batches was made both with and without the peel.

Cucumber Soap with French Green Clay

I added two teaspoons of clay to the basic recipe, using the juice from peeled cucumbers as the liquid. I thought the soap might be green, but it was pale beige. However, some green clays *are* green enough to affect final color, so if this is what you want in a clay soap, ask around and shop around.

Cucumber and Apricot Soap

15.9 ounces (451 grams) apricot kernel oil
3 ounces (85 grams) shea butter
2.1 ounces (59 grams) castor oil
9 ounces (255 grams) palm kernel oil flakes
10.6 ounces (300 grams) frozen cucumber juice
4.2 ounces (119 grams) lye

Cucumber and Avocado Soap

6 ounces (171 grams) avocado butter
9 ounces (255 grams) coconut oil
15 ounces (425 grams) olive oil
10 ounces (283 grams) frozen cucumber puree or juice
4.2 ounces (119 grams) lye

I used a mixture of frozen puree and juice in my batch.

Color—Natural and Artificial

The natural color of my cucumber soap is pure white when it's made with juice of peeled cucumbers and medium green olive oil.

Soaps with juice from peeled cucumbers, olive oil, and 76-degree coconut oil are light beige unless they're warmed during setting. Those darken somewhat. Including the peel with the juice also makes a darker beige soap, not green.

Made with cucumber puree, soaps might be either beige or pale green. Regardless of the main color, if the cucumbers aren't peeled, the soap has green flecks.

In my batches, the only green soap was the one with cucumber I pureed in a food processor. When I pureed the cucumber with the stick blender, I got beige soap with green flecks.

In the batches I tried to swirl, I used green chrome oxide for the color. It didn't bleed and was quite stable. However, in the darker batches, the contrast wasn't enough for a particularly good effect. For best results with color effects, use juice from peeled cucumbers and don't let the soap gel. Some of my swirl batches traced and set too quickly for swirling to work well.

Hardness

Many of my cucumber soaps tended to be soft. I suggest making cucumber soaps with an oil mix that has at least a medium hardness value, and with superfatting at no more than 5%.

Does Cucumber Accelerate Trace?

I'd heard that cucumber fragrance, or cucumber melon fragrance, accelerates trace. None of the ones I tried actually did. Neither did the cucumber itself.

What Would I Do?

If I were making cucumber soap for myself, I'd use the strained juice rather than pulp. I preferred the texture of those soaps. Or I'd use a 50-50 combination of yogurt and strained cucumber juice for the liquid.

If I wanted the green flecks of cucumber peel, I'd process the peel in a food processor with water, drain it, and add it to my soap at trace.

For making juice, I preferred the results I got using a heavy-duty vegetable juicer to what my food processor was able to do. I believe almost any fruit or vegetable juice could be used in soap this way, although I have tried only a few. For any organic liquid such as vegetable juice, I'd work with it frozen.

Since vegetable juices tend to be acidic, I'd use them in soap formulations with good hardness and would not have my liquid exceed 30% of the weight of the fats. I would not formulate for superfatting above 5%.

For more thoughts about developing your own recipes, see October.

Low Temperature Soapmaking

Throughout history, soap has mostly been made hot. In fact, soapmakers were known as "soap boilers." Like many professions, soap boiling had its patron saint—Saint Florian, who is also the patron saint of firefighters.

Saint Florian's Gate, Poland

As far as I've been able to learn, high temperature work was the rule both for family and commercial soapmaking until around 1940. At that time, companies who manufactured lye began to market it differently for private soapmaking, which was falling out of fashion. I've found the term "cold process soapmaking" in an undated lye company pamphlet that appears to be from about 1940-1950, based on the illustrations.

What we call hot process soapmaking for craft soapmakers today may take one of a number of forms. The soap may be brought to trace without heat, then cooked in a slow cooker. Or it may be brought to trace without heat, poured into a mold, and "baked" at low temperature in an oven. Or it may be heated prior to trace.

Cold process isn't actually cold. It may be done at anything from room temperature to about 120°F (49°C). Typically, the soap is poured into molds and kept at room temperature until it sets, then unmolded, sliced, and set aside for curing.

What are the advantages, hot or cold? Hot process is ready to use almost immediately, is kinder to additives, and requires less fragrance/essential oil.

Cold process is faster (not counting curing time), may be easier to mold, and may have less fumes and require less direct supervision.

Both methods also have disadvantages. Some soapmakers use only one, some use both, depending on the ingredients they're using.

Milk soapmakers came up with a special technique I refer to as Cool Technique in my book *Milk Soapmaking*. In this method, the soapmaking liquid is frozen. Lye is trickled onto it, and the heat from the dissolving lye gradually melts the ice. The soap is mixed normally and may be refrigerated or even briefly put into a freezer after pouring to keep the heat of saponification from scorching milk or other fragile ingredients.

Like other methods, Cool Technique has its advantages and disadvantages. Preventing scorching is its main advantage. It also reduces fumes—a lot.

But if you count freezing time, it takes longer. Also, Cool Technique soaps may be more likely to get the chalky white deposits known as soda ash (For ideas about preventing and removing soda ash, see November.)

If you make many different kinds of soap, it's probably an advantage to consider all techniques, and to be skilled in all.

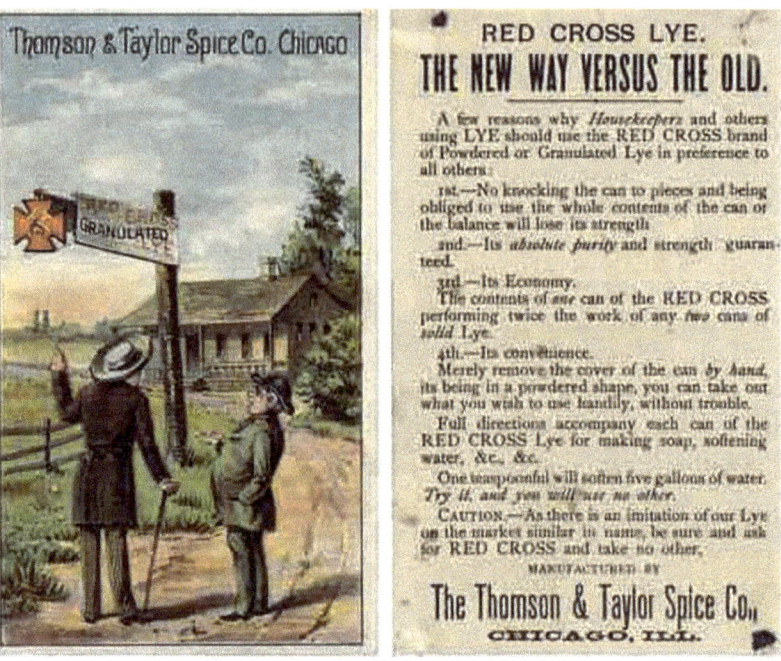

Nineteenth-century trade card promoting the use of manufactured lye for soapmaking. We don't know how the soap was made, but availability of a standardized manufactured product would have been a major advantage over homemade lye.

Pamphlet for use of Gillett Brand lye in home soapmaking. It's undated, but based on the dress and hairstyle of the model, I'm guessing it was published around 1940–1950. It uses the term "cold process soapmaking."

JULY

CITRUS SOAPS

Soapmaking as a Business

Citrus in Soapmaking—Why?

Lemon juice is an old beauty treatment, believed to help heal blemishes and whiten the skin. It's touted as a moisturizer, exfoliant, and toner. The same claims have been made more recently for orange peel.

Whether citrus has any real effect on skin or not, its fragrance is delightful. Citrus scents are among the most popular for soap. Citrus essential oils are notorious for fading, though, and many vendors' products are weak to begin with.

The citrus soaps I experimented with all had excellent lather, possibly because of the sugar in the juice they were made with. I used Cool Technique for these soaps to prevent scorching the sugar in the juice.

Most soaps I made with the fruit juice for liquid had a pleasant orange color. Again, the lack of scorching from the lye probably helped keep the color clear and fresh, so this is another advantage of using Cool Technique.

Not surprisingly, any use of peel, even finely ground peel, will result in a gardener's soap or scrub soap. If the peel is dried before use, it's much scrubbier. In my experiments, I thought some of the soaps were too rough, although my gardening friends liked them. Peel—especially the finely powdered peel—did seem to help stabilize the scent, but the texture may not be what you want.

Fading and Citrus Essential Oils

Citrus essential oils are notorious for fading in cold process soap. I experimented with many of them and found that their stability varies quite a bit, depending on their strength and quality to begin with.

I thought they might be more stable if I used Cool Technique soapmaking, but low temperature didn't increase the stability of the EOs.

A number of sources recommended using may chang (litsea cubeba), vetiver, lemongrass, lemon myrtle, or lemon eucalyptus to stabilize citrus essential oils. I didn't try everything suggested, but of the ones I did try, I was most satisfied with lemongrass.

Contrary to popular ideas, citrus oils are not reactive with lye or other soap ingredients. Reactivity is not the reason they fade.

Basic Citrus Soap and Variations

- 12 ounces (340 grams) coconut oil
- 6 ounces (170 grams) olive oil
- 12 ounces (340 grams) sunflower oil
- 9 ounces (255 grams) liquid (citrus juice, citrus juice mixed with another liquid, or citrus juice mixed with milk, cream, or yogurt)
- 4.3 ounces (124 grams) lye

Optional additions: citrus peel (either powdered or ground), citrus essential oil, citrus fragrance, supplementary fragrance or essential oils, oatmeal, honey.

Orange Yogurt Soap with Peel

This soap was extremely popular with my testers. It has great lather. The peel makes it a scrub soap.

The liquid was a 50-50 mixture of fresh orange juice and whole milk yogurt, mixed together before freezing. I used 1.6 ounces of 10× orange essential oil for the fragrance. I also added about a tablespoon of pulverized dried orange peel that had soaked overnight in more of the orange EO.

Orange Yogurt Soap with Peel

Lemon and Honey Soap

Use the basic recipe. For liquid, make a 50-50 mix of yogurt and water. Add one tablespoon honey. Mix very well—I used a food processor. Freeze.

I used a mixture of lemon essential oil and lemon verbena fragrance in this batch.

This version traced and set quickly, which wasn't the case with the other variation of the basic recipe. I've used the fragrance before without trace acceleration, so it wasn't that either. I believe the accelerant must have been the honey.

Lemon and Honey Soap

Texas Ruby Red Grapefruit Soap

Even with the addition of litsea and lemongrass, the grapefruit scent did not hold well. Either a stronger essential oil or a fragrance oil might improve it.

       9 ounces (255 grams) coconut oil
       7.5 ounces (213 grams) avocado oil
       3 ounces (85 grams) sunflower oil
       10.5 ounces (298 grams) olive oil
       1 tablespoon pulverized grapefruit peel
       9 ounces (255 grams) frozen ruby red grapefruit juice
       4.2 ounces (120 grams) lye

For scent, I used a blend of 2 ounces grapefruit EO, .3 ounces lemongrass EO, and .25 ounces litsea EO.

Lemongrass, Coconut, and Almond Soap

This soap has no fruit juice, because I wanted to see what role the juice might have in color, scent, and lathering. The result was good lather, especially creamy, and a paler color than any of the fruit juice soaps. The color did change in the first 24 hours, becoming somewhat darker and more orange. So, at least part of the warm color of the juice soaps is caused by the essential oil, not the juice.

The scent was a blend of lemongrass essential oil and mint essential oil. At least in the early stages of curing, I couldn't pick out the mint as a separate scent. The lemongrass essential oil seems more stable in soap than any of the others, except possibly the bergamot.

> 10.5 ounces (298 grams) sweet almond oil
> 10.5 ounces (298 grams) unsalted dairy butter or ghee
> 9 ounces (255 grams) coconut oil
> 9 ounces (255 grams) frozen plain coconut milk
> 4.5 ounces (129 grams) lye

Many soapmakers overlook dairy butter as a potential soapmaking fat, but it works quite well. However, butter does have an odor, as do many other unrefined fats. From one batch to another, the odor varies from negligible to unacceptable, and I never succeeded in pinning down the factor that caused the problems, much to my frustration.

My experiments with dairy butter should be regarded as just that—experiments. It was very successful for me with this lemongrass soap, less so with a lavender EO soap I made on another occasion. The texture of butter soap is outstanding.

Creamy Orange Soap

Supposedly, bergamot fixes the scent of orange. It's a citrus-like fragrance. I suspect it adds more citrus scent *without* fixing any. I also found I don't particularly care for the scent of bergamot. It's just different enough from orange that it smells "off" to me.

The scent was more stable than orange essential oil, even the 10× orange EO.

The orange peel powder produced a slightly gritty texture, so addition of peel—even very fine powder—will give you a scrub soap. It's possible that the powdered orange peel helped make the orange fragrance of this soap more stable. It's definitely lasting longer than most of the other citrus soaps in this experiment.

> 1 tablespoon orange peel powder
> 3 ounces 10× orange essential oil
> .5 ounces bergamot essential oil
> 9 ounces (255 grams) half and half (light cream), frozen
> 2.1 ounces (60 grams) orange juice, frozen
> 6 ounces (170 grams) peanut oil
> 9 ounces (255 grams) coconut oil
> 15 ounces (425 grams) olive oil
> 4.2 ounces (119 grams) lye

Mix the orange peel powder with the essential oils several hours before making your soap. The half and half and orange juice may be combined before freezing.

What Would I Do?

    If I were using citrus EOs in soap, I'd greatly prefer 10× orange or lemongrass to any of the others I tried for this project.

    I don't particularly favor coarse scrub soaps, so I'd use commercial orange peel powder over any of the homemade citrus peel I made. Orange peel seems to harden a bit as the soap is used, and with coarser peel, the scrub effect can get harsher than I like.

Soapmaking as a Business

    I'm often asked about turning a soapmaking hobby into a business. I actually went the other way—started off apprenticing to a professional soapmaker, ran my own business, then decided after a year or two to drop back to hobby status. And then, of course, I also decided to write about what I'd learned and figured out.

    Since writing my first soapmaking books—*Smart Soapmaking* and *Milk Soapmaking*—I'm proud to say that quite a few of my readers have become successful professionals. Not that I take much credit for this. I might have given their boat one little push away from the dock, but they're the ones who've been paddling and steering it ever since.

    So, I don't pretend to be a professional soapmaker. I'm a writer who makes soap. But I do have some observations, based on friends' experience and my own.

Know Your Market and Develop your Marketing Abilities

    When I was in business, I was very naive about marketing. I expected the soaps, if they were good enough, to almost sell themselves—aided by good packaging, of course. Looking back, some of my mistakes were quite funny.

    I went to a Christmas fair one year with soaps I'd made on a Nutcracker Ballet theme. There was Spanish Chocolate, Arabian Coffee, Sugar Plum, Chinese Green Tea, Snowflake—the whole cast. They were nice soaps. But I wasn't offering them to a particularly arty crowd. Very few people were interested.

JULY

The Sugar Plum Fairy is a poor soap salesman!

Another failure had to do with packaging. I kept hearing about how packaging made a difference. So, I bought a number of beautiful baskets from Amish people in Wisconsin.

They were miniature melon baskets, just the right size to hold a bar of soap and a matching lotion, or two bars of soap—small gift sets. They were inexpensive too, and added only about three dollars to the price of the set. They came in natural as well as lovely colors. And they were keepsake quality. (The photo shows what they looked like, though this one isn't miniature.)

But they didn't sell. Three dollars is three dollars. I gave away beautiful baskets for years.

Beautiful packaging, no sale. My mini-melon baskets were lovely, but they didn't add value to my soaps and lotions.

I tried joining a local chamber of commerce and participating in their activities. This wasn't effective. Neither was giving samples, either in person or through the mail.

A good part of building your business is figuring out what *doesn't* work and getting rid of it.

Know Your Competition

If you're in a market with many competitors, how will you stand out? It's sad to go to a farmers' market with three or four soap vendors. None of them are making enough for their effort and investment to be worthwhile.

On the other hand, if there's a market opening up that you discover or create for yourself, you may have fairly smooth sailing. But don't go into a soapmaking business blind.

Do Your Homework

Any online bookseller or library will have many current books on craft businesses. Find and study them. There are even a few books specifically on soapmaking as a business. And at least one computer program for pricing and inventory control in a soapmaking business.

Know the laws in your area. Get the licenses and permits you need. Follow all laws about labeling, taxes, and fees.

Get insurance.

Don't Jump In Too Soon

Unless you're working under the supervision of an experienced soapmaker, please don't start selling as soon as you've made a batch or two. It takes a while to get consistent quality and to have responsible confidence that your product is safe.

Resources

Handcrafted Soap and Cosmetic Guild—More resources for craft business soapmakers than I could possibly mention, including affordable insurance.
Soap and Cosmetic Labeling and *Good Manufacturing Practices* by Marie Gale
SoapMaker—Windows app
Making Soap, Cosmetics & Candles (formerly *Saponifier Magazine*)

AUGUST
HERBAL SOAPS
Working with Trace Accelerants

Herbs in Soapmaking—Why?

Washington State lavender farm

Almost everyone likes herbs. How well they work in soapmaking is another matter. There are different ways to go about it.

• Infuse the oils with fresh or dried herbs. There are several ways to do this, using either heat or time to transfer the herb fragrance to the oil.

• Make an herbal tea and use that as your liquid.

• Herb essential oils are available for a few herbs. They vary in strength, holding power, and attractiveness as scent. Some are less suitable for solo use than for adding complexity in blending.

Herb fragrances don't produce an all-natural soap. In my experience, some also are unsatisfactory as scents, unless you want soap that smells like spaghetti sauce. Fragrances like Herbal Essence don't smell so much like food but are "green" floral blends that don't reproduce any particular herb.

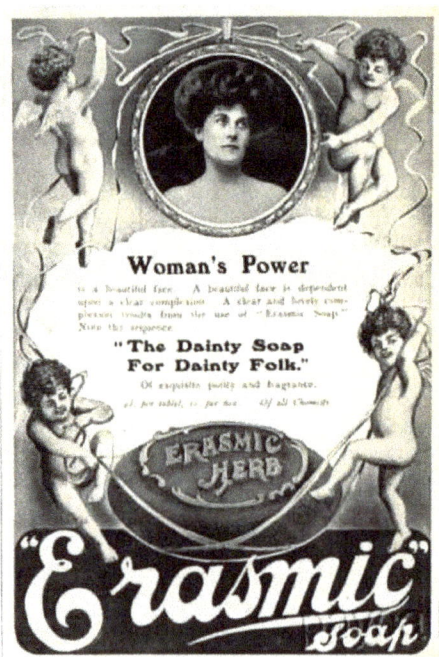

1907 ad for herbal soap

Botanicals in Soap

Pay attention to the properties of herbs when designing your soap. It may not make much sense to design a soothing chamomile or calendula soap and then put a lot of scrubby material in it. Or to put soothing herbs into an oil mixture that's more cleansing than emollient. Look at the whole picture.

It may look nice to put a lot of botanicals into a soap, but that stuff is going to end up in your bathwater, or at least in your drain.

One leaf that supposedly works well to give a green speckle appearance is passionflower leaf. This is available in tea form. (Note: I haven't been able to find just the leaf. Passiflora tea turns out to be the flowers). Another is dried parsley.

When you've decorated the top of a loaf or block of soap with botanicals, cut from the bottom up when you cut it into bars. If you cut from the top down, you'll drag the botanicals down through the soap.

Infusing Oils with Herbs

Mint, from old herbal

You'll come across many different suggestions for doing this. Almost all are intended for cooking or salad oil use, and most work well for that.

After a number of experiments with infusing oils for soapmaking, I only found one method that worked well for me. That is to add commercial dried herbs to oil and leave it to steep in a cool dark place for a fairly long time—a month or more. When I tried infusing oil with fresh or home-dried herbs, I got mold.

I've read that herbs can be infused by simmering the herb and oil mixture in a slow cooker. For me, this produced scorched oil.

I've also read that it's possible to infuse oils with herbs in much the same way you'd make sun tea—put the mixture into a clear glass jar and set it in the sun for a while. I believe it, but my part of the world doesn't get enough direct sunlight to make this practical, so I didn't test it.

Herb Teas

All kinds of herb teas are available—mostly in tea bags, in my supermarket, but some are packaged as loose tea. Chamomile, mint, lavender, and many others are easy to find. I wondered whether herb teas would give any scent or color to the finished soap, and if they did, how long it would last. I also wondered if herb teas would affect the feel and texture of the soap.

With all the choices available, there was no way to test them all, but I selected a few for the experiments here.

Herb Essential Oils and Fragrances

Common thyme, from a old herbal

Essential Oils

An essential oil is a volatile oil that contains the aroma compounds from a plant. EOs are usually steam-distilled, solvent-extracted, or cold-pressed. I've seen articles on "making your own essential oils" that describe *infusing* oils with herbs, but it's not the same thing. Essential oils are much more concentrated and fragrant than infused oils.

Lavender and rosemary are popular. Bay laurel, catnip, sage, fennel, chamomile, mint, marjoram, basil, and thyme are also available. When using herbal essential oils, it's wise to research possible medicinal effects, since they're very concentrated. Responsible vendors may warn about use of specific essential oils during pregnancy, or with certain medical conditions, but it's a good idea to do your own investigating—many of the drugs in our modern pharmacopeia originated with herbs and other plants.

Some herb essential oils accelerate trace dramatically, and not all vendors mention this in their catalogs. Other essential oils seemed to retard trace. Ask at the time of purchase about an essential oil's behavior in CP soap, or begin with a very small test batch, or both. Test a blend in any case, because a combination of essential oils can have an effect that none of them do by themselves. The scent of a mixture in the finished soap may also be different from what you'd expect, judging from before they're saponified.

Some herb essential oils are quite expensive. Others are much more affordable. Quality varies a lot from one vendor to another. When you're shopping for herb essential oils, first buy the smallest size possible, especially if the EO is a pricey one, then decide whether it's worth the money. Once a vendor gives you a specific product you like, stick with that.

I made one blend of herb essential oils that was a standout: 43% bay, 21% sage, 7% thyme, and 29% rosemary. Be warned, though: It accelerates trace. (Both bay and thyme EOs are accelerants). See suggestions below for working with accelerated trace.

Old medicinal herb boxes, shown with a selection of herbal soaps. Uses are listed on the sides of the boxes—many herbs are effective medicines.

Fragrance Oils

Fragrance oils are artificial, of course, so I'll only touch on them in this discussion of herbal soaps. I've tried a few herb fragrances that are billed as duplicating essential oils. I didn't think any of them were convincing. Some "herbal" fragrances are really floral fragrances with "green" notes. They're pleasant, but not the pure scent of herbs.

Coconut-Almond Soap scented with herbal fragrance oil

Botanicals and Lye

Botanicals—actual plant material such as lavender buds—may be affected by lye.

However, not all the common information about this is reliable. When I began researching the effect of lye on botanicals in soapmaking, I ran into so many contradictions that I decided to do a little testing myself.

For instance, I found contradictory statements about adding dried mint leaves to CP soap. Some said the leaves turn black—that the best way to get the effect you want is to use dried parsley leaves, which remain green. Others said that mint is one of the few leaves that stays green. Yet another source said they "bleed"—and I wasn't sure what that meant.

Here are my test soaps with mint and parsley:

These soaps were made from the same basic recipe, given below. Both were scented with mint essential oil. The one on the left has dried mint leaves from an herbal teabag. The one on the right has culinary dried parsley.

Equal amounts by volume were added, but the mint was much finer, so there's a big difference in actual density, and probably in weight as well.

At first, the mint in the soap—though a duller green than the parsley—was the same color it was in the teabag. But after a few hours, the edges of the mint soap developed rusty brown spotting. This is apparently what "bleeding" meant! And the color spreads and darkens as the soap is used.

For a second try, I made mint tea with one of the teabags, squeezed out the leaves, and used them damp. I mixed them into the soap at trace, then poured into molds.

The rusty staining hasn't been completely eliminated, but there's much less. (It shows more in this photo than on the actual soap bar.) However, in use, it increased.

If you want green specks in the soap, with no risk of "bleeding," parsley is preferable—at least at first. In use, though, the parsley flakes harden, become scrubbier, and darken.

Calendula and a few other botanicals don't change in soap.

You can also avoid color change by applying the botanicals to the surface of the soap after pouring. If you do this with soap in a log mold, your addition will wind up all on one side of your bars. With tray or individual molds, it will cover one of the bar's larger surfaces. Either way, fill the mold slightly below the rim and press the botanical material into the surface gently as the soap is setting. (Of course, while doing this, you'll still be wearing gloves!)

Whether you're using a botanical throughout the soap or only on the surface, test a bar in use—sink, shower, and bathtub—before marketing it. If a soap is pretty but requires cleaning the tub every time it's used, you won't get many repeat customers for it.

Since there are obviously many more botanicals than I'm able to test, I recommend you experiment with them yourself, trying very small batches before going full scale. Once you've found a material, texture, and quantity you like, you're set.

Basic Herbal Soap and Variations

Here's a recipe you can use as the basis for an herbal soap. Just add the herbs, in whatever form you choose.

8 ounces (226 grams) shea butter
10 ounces (284 grams) coconut oil
12 ounces (340 grams) grapeseed oil
9 ounces (255 grams) water or other liquid
4.1 ounces (118 grams) lye

Two Basic Herbal soaps. The one on bottom was scented with sage essential oil, the one on top with a blend of fennel, lemongrass, and rosemary. No colorants were used—the difference in color is due to the colors of the EOs.

Olive Oil Variation

Replace the grapeseed oil with olive oil. Increase the lye to 4.2 ounces (121 grams). I was especially pleased with this variation. It had great lather, both bubbly and creamy.

With this mildly scented infused olive oil, neither the rosemary color nor its fragrance remained in the finished soap.

Lavender Cucumber Variation

Building on my June project, I decided to use frozen cucumber juice for the liquid. Use lavender essential oil, or a blend of herbal essential oils with lavender dominant. I also experimented with dairy butter as one of the fats.

Made in a block mold, this soap developed a bull's-eye at the center. If smooth color is important, make soaps with fragile ingredients like butter or cucumber juice in tray molds or individual molds.

I found dairy butter difficult to work with. The texture of the soap was superb, but some batches developed an odd odor, which is why I didn't give a recipe. It was particularly noticeable in combination with lavender essential oil. Substituting ghee for butter did not solve the problem.

AUGUST

Coconut Almond Soap with Herb Tea

Chamomile plant, from old herbal

21 ounces (595 grams) almond oil
9 ounces (255 grams) coconut oil
9 ounces (255 grams) frozen herb tea
4.3 ounces (123 grams) lye

The herb tea seemed to have little effect except for color, but the color was uneven. The blotchiness might not be a problem in a soap with leaf "speckles." It does show in a plain soap.

Chamomile Tea Variation—Neither the fragrance of the chamomile tea nor the color survived saponification. Slow to set, slow to cure. Beautiful lather.

Mint Tea Variation—When the lye was added to the tea, the liquid turned bright red. The color remained until the soap was poured into the molds—as the soap was setting, it faded to tan and then to a slightly blotchy yellow. It had a very faint mint smell at first, which quickly disappeared.

Tea soaps, mint (left) and chamomile (right)

Triple Calendula Soap

12.6 ounces (357 grams) calendula-infused sunflower oil
9.9 ounces (281 grams) palm kernel oil flakes
7.5 ounces (213 grams) shea butter
9 ounces (255 grams) water or calendula tea
4.0 ounces (114 grams) lye
Ground calendula (optional)
Calendula petals to decorate (optional)

Grind calendula flowers to add at trace if you want a scrubby soap. The amount would depend on how much "scrub" you want, but don't use more than four teaspoons of the ground petals for this amount of base oils. You can also use whole calendula petals in soap, instead of the ground petals. Soak the powder or petals in some of the base oil before using.

To make calendula tea to use for the liquid, pour boiling distilled water over calendula petals and let steep. Again, start with more than you need, to make up for waste. Strain, freeze, and use frozen as you would with milk soap.

To decorate the surface of the soap, first fill the molds slightly less than full. With your gloves still on, press calendula flowers into the exposed face of the soap as it's setting.

AUGUST

Tomato Basil Soap

10.5 ounces (298 grams) coconut oil
4.5 ounces (128 grams) avocado butter
11.4 ounces (323 grams) almond oil
3.6 ounces (102 grams) olive oil
9 ounces (255 grams) tomato juice, frozen
4.3 ounces (124 grams) lye
Sweet basil essential oil

I used juice I'd made myself in a juicer. Not sure if canned or bottled tomato juice would give the same results.

Sweet basil essential oil is very strong. If using it alone, you'd want less than an ounce for this amount of soap.

The soap was slow to trace, slow to set. This might be a good choice for soaps with special effects, where you need some time.

When the bars were about half set, I gently smoothed dried parsley flakes into the top of the soap.

If you use fragrance oils, you could add one of the tomato leaf oils to this one. Or blend with one of the citrus essential oils. Or for a kitchen scrub soap, add lemon or orange peel powder.

Lavender, Shea, and Almond Soap

10.5 ounces (298 grams) almond oil
10.2 ounces (289 grams) coconut oil
9.3 ounces (264 grams) shea butter
1.6 ounces (45 grams) lavender essential oil
9 ounces (255 grams) light cream or half-and-half, frozen
4.3 ounces (122 grams) lye
Lavender buds to sprinkle on top, if desired

The lavender buds on the surface are pretty, but they do dry out and become brown in time. I wouldn't add them to another batch.

Working with Accelerants

Bay Laurel—I love bay leaves in food and love the essential oil in soap. But it is a fierce trace accelerant, and it's necessary to use every trick I know to make soap successfully with it. It's only worth it to take so much trouble for a real favorite.

We say that certain materials accelerate trace, but that's only part of the picture. They accelerate everything—trace, setting, and the rate at which the soap's pH drops to a usable level. In the process, they generate a lot of heat, even after the soap is poured. So, you not only have to avoid the proverbial "soap on a stick," you also have to think about "volcanoes," scorching of oils or other ingredients, or cracking as the soap sets and cures.

You need to consider both the starting temperature and the way that heat can build up after the soap is poured. Saponification generates heat all by itself, so the soap can get hot on its own after you pour it into molds.

I avoid fragrance oils that accelerate trace, but some essential oils do, too, and if you want their scent, you have to learn to work with them. Here are a number of pointers for working with accelerants. Don't worry—you won't try them all in the same batch! They're offered as ideas to consider—not all personally tested by me.

- Work cooler. Use frozen liquid and/or chilled liquid fats.
- Let melted solid fats cool as much as possible. One way to do this is to mix them with the liquid fats. The whole mixture is less likely to solidify at room temperature.
- When working cold, avoid using a high percentage of hard fats, as false trace is possible if fats congeal before they're emulsified.
- Increase liquid. My recipes have water or other liquid at 30% of oil weight, but liquid can be increased to as much as 38%.
- Don't use fragile liquids like milk that can't take higher temperatures.
- Avoid using honey, sugar, or sugar-containing liquids such as fruit juice for part or all of the soap's liquid.
- Avoid using alcoholic liquids.
- Use slow-tracing oils such as olive oil. Avoid oils such as castor that accelerate trace by themselves.
- Use less of the trace-accelerating essential oil, or combine it with others that retard trace or don't affect it.
- Keep quantities down. The more soap you make at once, the more heat is generated, even normally. With an accelerant in the mix, it's easy to generate too much heat.
- Use tray molds or individual molds to prevent heat buildup after pouring.
- Use molds made of a material that transfers heat quickly. Silicone or plastic would be good. Wood molds retain heat, and are less desirable.
- Don't insulate the molds.

- Hand stir, at least part of the time.
- Mix the accelerant into the soap *after* pouring. This would be easiest in a silicone block mold or loaf mold—it's best to use one with smooth surfaces rather than a pattern or ripple in the bottom, since it's harder to stir quickly and thoroughly in a patterned mold. To do this, mix the essential oil or other accelerating ingredient with a little of the base oil and set aside. Mix other ingredients as usual until the soap is well mixed but not yet at trace. Pour into the mold and add the accelerant mixture. Hand stir until trace is reached. Stir thoroughly and carefully, paying special attention to edges and corners. (A spatula is useful for this.) Since the block mold shape will retain heat, this idea should probably be combined with cooling the mold as the soap sets.
- Refrigerate molds after pouring as we do with milk soaps.
- If you're using more than one mold, don't place them close together after pouring—this makes the soap retain heat, and can cause a "volcano." Set them down with air space around them.
- Mix a small amount of one of the liquid fats in the soap with the trace-accelerating essential oil. Add after the other soap ingredients are well mixed and slightly emulsified.
- A mixture with an accelerant is probably not a good choice for swirling or fancy effects.
- If you really love an EO or FO that accelerates trace, consider making the soap with hot process technique instead of cold process.
- Be especially careful when you work with trace accelerants. It's possible for undissolved lye to remain in the mixture. Look at your soap critically, and test any "different" areas with pH paper, NOT WITH YOUR TONGUE OR FINGERS. Don't touch your soap until you've tested it. Look at the exterior of a soap log carefully before slicing, and test at different spots on the exterior. Look at the faces of the slices just as carefully. If you have individual bars, look all of them over thoroughly, and test any areas that look different.

What Would I Do?

If I wanted to use a trace-accelerating FO or EO in a soap, I'd do some or all of the following.
- Work cold.
- Increase liquid to 35% of fats rather than my typical 30%.
- Avoid other ingredients such as sugars that tend to accelerate trace.
- Use a silicone block mold.
- Add the accelerant after pouring the soap mixture into the mold.
- Cool the soap after pouring.

SEPTEMBER

OATMEAL SOAPS

Selecting Vendors

Oatmeal in Soapmaking—Why?

Oatmeal soap is very popular at markets and craft fairs. My friends who sell soap report that this one does well year after year. But exactly what is oatmeal soap, and why do we use oatmeal in soap?

First of all, many "oatmeal soaps" aren't actually made with oatmeal. They may be decorated with a light sprinkling of rolled oats, but basically, they're plain soap with an Oatmeal, Milk, and Honey fragrance, sometimes with an added touch of cinnamon fragrance. It's very appealing. But it's not really oatmeal soap.

Soaps have been made with oatmeal or oat milk for a long time, though, and the belief is that it's good for the skin. It's variously said to be good for oily skin, dry skin, skin irritations, the skin's acid mantle, and shingles; to be exfoliant, antibiotic, and anti-acne; and so on. But if you're selling soap, be careful not to make claims that violate labeling regulations. (Marie Gale's excellent book on Soap and Cosmetic Labeling can help here.)

Since I'm not a dermatologist, I can't say what oatmeal does for skin. Based on my own experience, I found oatmeal soaps to be rather drying.

In any event, oatmeal is very popular as a soap ingredient and scent.

Rolled Oats and Oat Flour

I've read recommendations to use hydrolyzed oats, baby oatmeal, instant oatmeal, and ordinary rolled oats in soap. When I checked the labels on hydrolyzed oats and baby oatmeal, the brands that were available to me had too many wild-card additives. I used rolled oats to make my oat milk, and bought oat flour to incorporate in soap as an exfoliant.

I wouldn't exceed one tablespoon of oat flour per pound of base oils. Soap can get soft and doughy if it has too much oatmeal in it. Oat flour didn't make my soaps "scrubby" the way some other additions will.

Some soapmakers soak dry ingredients like rolled oats and oat flour in some of the base oil for several hours before making soap. I tried it and didn't find it made much difference in my batches.

It's a good idea to be aware of temperature when using rolled oats or oat flour in soap. Depending on the size and shape of the mold, the soap may overheat as it's curing, to the point of forming a bull's-eye. Especially the first time you use a particular recipe in a particular mold, monitor the temperature, and if the soap seems to be getting hot, refrigerate it to slow it down.

Or, if you're fairly sure you're likely to get a soap that heats quickly—for example, if you're using a log mold—put the mold in the freezer after pouring. I freeze it for two hours for a two-pound (oils) batch. A larger batch might require more chilling.

Honey and Beeswax

Honey, like any sugar, accelerates trace. It can also make soap turn brown.

When I use honey, I add it to the liquid, mix very well, and freeze them together. This helps to prevent browning and slows trace somewhat—but don't count on it. Any time you use an accelerant of any kind, be prepared to move quickly.

Also, keep honey amounts fairly low, to prevent stickiness and veins or blobs of honey in the finished soap. About 5% of the base oil weight is about as high as I'd go.

Keep an eye on soap with any fragile ingredient like honey in it. Sugars will contribute to overheating, so monitor your soap carefully.

Oatmeal soap may tend to be on the soft side, so you may choose to add a little beeswax. Beeswax melts at a higher temperature than most fats, and it's flammable. It has to be handled with care. It's also difficult to clean off of things.

Buy the beeswax in pastilles and start melting them several hours in advance of soapmaking. Fill a half-pint mason jar a quarter full of the pastilles and cover it. Put about two inches of water into the crock of a slow cooker and set it on Low. Put in the jar of beeswax and cover the crock. When you're ready to make soap, the beeswax is melted, and it's easy to remove the amount you want with a spoon. Don't try to clean out the jar, just keep it for the next time, adding more pastilles as needed.

Liquids—Milk, Cream, and Oat Milk

I've never figured the fat content of milk in my lye calculation. I don't even figure cream. If that means I have a little extra superfatting, so be it. I've never had a problem doing it this way, but if you do want to include it, you have to determine how many grams of milk fat are in your liquid. Ordinary milk is about 4% fat. Cream varies by brand and type, but the package should say. I don't use cream over 30% milk fat.

Then you do the math to see how much milk fat to list in your lye calculator.

You can easily make oat milk, and I prefer that to the commercial product, which may have additives like sugar and stabilizers.

Both oat and dairy milk should be used frozen. With dairy products, expect odd colors and odors while mixing. With higher-fat products, the lye mixture may be thick. This is normal.

I haven't detected any odd odors with oat milk, but as it melts and combines with the lye, gelatinous blobs form. I ignore them. They seem to be smoothed out by the stick blender. Anyway, they disappear.

Milk, oat milk, and cream may also be likely to overheat. So, treat the same as recommended for honey, above.

Make oat milk by combining one part rolled oats with eight parts room-temperature distilled water. (That would be half a cup of oats to one quart water.) Let this mixture sit for fifteen or twenty minutes. Process in a blender or with your stick blender. Strain. (I used a "nut milk bag," but a clean flour sack towel or a fine strainer would do.) Or if you prefer to use steel cut oats, use one part oats to three parts water, and proceed exactly the same way.

Not everyone reacts to the fumes of milk soap, but if you do, they'll give you a sore throat. Use good ventilation. Of course, you should do that with *all* soapmaking—but if milk soap is a problem for you, use even *better* ventilation.

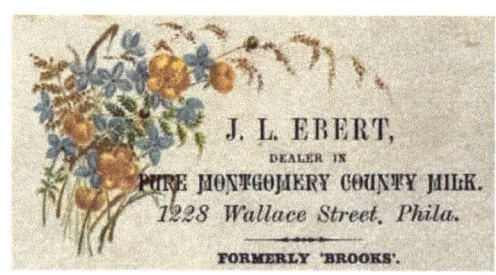

Cinnamon and Other Spices

Spices are delightful. Fragrant, warming, comforting. It's easy to see why the Silk Road of early days was also the Spice Road. Almost everyone loves spices.

But the real thing is a skin irritant. Use ground spices very sparingly—no more than half a teaspoon per pound of base oils, if that. Use cinnamon essential oil in accordance with the vendor's recommendations. Or use a fragrance oil instead of an essential oil or ground spices.

Oatmeal, Milk, and Honey Fragrance Oils

These vary a lot from different vendors. Some smell lovely, others are reminiscent of Play-Doh. All the OMH fragrance oils I've tried contain vanilla, and so will turn the soap brown.

Basic Oatmeal Soap and Variations

Here's a recipe you can use as the basis for different oatmeal soaps, along with some possible variations.

    21 ounces (595 grams) olive oil
    9 ounces (255 grams) coconut oil
    9 ounces (255 grams) frozen liquid—oat milk, milk, chocolate milk, buttermilk, diluted yogurt, cream, or water
    4.2 ounces (121 grams) lye

Use Cool Technique for mixing.

If you use yogurt, dilute 50-50 with distilled water, or more if you use Greek yogurt. I use natural whole milk yogurt, not lowfat. Don't use flavored yogurt—it has too much sugar and is likely to make the soap overheat.

Basic recipe, using chocolate milk for the liquid and no added coloring. The chocolate contributes very little color. The soap has excellent creamy lather.

Variations

• Add up to ¾ ounce (20 grams) of honey to the milk before freezing. Make sure it's very well mixed.

• Add up to 1½ teaspoons cinnamon to the oil before adding the lye. Mix well with your stick blender.

• Add up to 1½ tablespoons of oat flour or coarsely chopped rolled oats just before trace.

• If desired, decorate the top with a light sprinkling of rolled oats. (This looks nice, but the oats are very scrubby—and they are going to end up down the drain.)

Basic recipe decorated with rolled oats. While the topping is attractive, the oats don't wash off quickly, and they tend to become hardened as the soap is used. I have heard complaints that toppings such as this can attract insects to the stored soap.

Oatmeal, Wheat Germ, and Buttermilk Soap

This soap has a very rich lather. Use only wheat germ oil that's refined, to avoid a vitamin pill odor in your soap.

1.5 ounces (43 grams) refined wheat germ oil
16.2 ounces (459 grams) olive oil
3 ounces (85 grams) almond oil
.3 ounces (8 grams) beeswax
9 ounces (255 grams) coconut oil
1 tablespoon oat flour or rolled oats
9 ounces (255 grams) buttermilk, frozen
4.2 ounces (120 grams) lye

Freeze buttermilk. Melt coconut oil and beeswax and combine with wheat germ oil, olive oil, and almond oil.

Proceed as for any Cool Technique soap. Cover and set in freezer for about two hours for a block mold, 45 minutes to an hour for a tray or individual molds.

Refrigerate a log mold overnight, a tray mold for several hours. Remove from refrigerator when spontaneous heat buildup stops.

Set in freezer again briefly before unmolding.

What Would I Do?

For my own use, I'd go fairly easy on oatmeal as an additive. It's noticeably drying. Of course, if you want that, it would be perfect.

I would not care to use any Oatmeal, Milk, and Honey fragrance I've ever tried. I think I'd use a cinnamon fragrance instead, or no fragrance.

Selecting Vendors

I get many, many questions about selecting vendors, and about the vendors I use personally. I have a Soapmaking Suppliers page on my web site—a sort of "yellow pages" guide—and I always give that link.

However, there really is a little more to it than that.

Online Vendors

One thing to consider is that you want to choose a vendor who is as close to you as possible, all other things being equal. Soapmaking supplies are often heavy and expensive to ship.

Compare prices. *And* compare quality.

Some vendors are better sources for smaller quantities. Others have much lower unit prices, but larger minimum quantities. Buy for your needs—oils and butters don't last indefinitely.

Pay attention to "blends." Especially with the more expensive butters, some vendors sell blends of the named butter with other fats. They label them honestly, but it's still easy to get confused.

Soapmaking supply vendors are by far the best source for fragrance oils and essential oils. The quality is better than what you get in a health food store or craft store, the price is far lower, and fragrance oils are more likely to be skin safe and appropriate for soap and lotion use.

I get pH strips and some soap molds from Amazon. They do tend to have everything.

"Brick and Mortar" Stores

Some supplies are easily available locally. Check big box stores, chain grocery stores, and restaurant supply stores for common fats such as olive oil, shortening, coconut oil, and lard. Depending on shipping costs, less common oils such as almond, hazelnut, and walnut may still be cheaper in local markets, health food stores, or gourmet stores than they would be if bought online and shipped.

In some states, you can get lye in hardware stores.

Restaurant supply stores and hardware stores are often good sources for cheap stainless steel cookware and utensils. And you do want the cheap pots—expensive ones are made to retain and distribute heat in cooking, and you need the opposite in soapmaking. For more thoughts on equipment, see January .

OCTOBER
BEER AND WINE SOAPS
Experimenting and Developing Recipes

Beer and Wine in Soapmaking—Why?

October is a harvest month, of course, and is also the month of Oktoberfest, a traditional celebration of the brewer's art in Germany.

Beer and wine have been increasingly popular for soap. As far as I can tell, that's a modern development. As fascinated as I am with antique soap advertisements, I've never run across one for beer or wine soap.

The sugars and carbs in beer and wine make good lather. Also, beer and wine soap may sell very well in some markets.

Experimenting—Why?

I'm probably the only on-call soapmaking author. Anyone can find me from my books or my web page. I answer email pretty quickly, too, so word gets around.

And I get calls for help—almost never, I'm proud to say, from readers who have closely followed the directions in my books. But soapmakers are creative people—they want to branch out, try something new, something that's their own.

So far, great. But the emails that make my heart sink are the ones where someone has had a large or disastrous failure. They've made ten pounds of soap, and it didn't set. Or it boiled over. Or it was just bad soap. Something that seemed like a good idea didn't turn out so well.

Sometimes, people ask ahead of time. This makes me happy. If I can point out things that will cause problems *before* someone commits time, money, and love to that project, and suggest modifications that will make it work, that makes my day.

This month gives a lot of attention to experimenting, and to developing something of your own in a methodical way that *will* work.

Using Alcoholic Beverages in Soapmaking

If you freeze the liquid, you don't have to add the lye as slowly as if you use it without freezing. If you don't freeze it, you have to trickle the lye into it a few grains at a time, or it's likely to erupt in a "volcano"—and even if not, it may overheat and boil over at the end anyway. With frozen liquid, you can add the lye fairly quickly. Some soapmakers don't freeze beer and wine, but it's safer to do it, and you avoid scorching.

Some soapmakers remove the alcohol from wine and beer because they don't want alcohol in their soap. They consider it drying. This may be true—I haven't found it to be a problem, but I encourage you to experiment and see what you think. See suggestions later in this month for experimenting and developing recipes.

Wine may freeze unevenly, with the water content of the wine becoming more solid than the rest. Since I freeze liquids in ice cube trays, I don't worry about this—I'll get the whole thing even if it separates somewhat. Beer freezes well, even if it's not cooked to remove the alcohol. For wine, this may depend somewhat on the alcohol content. With the 12% alcohol table wines I tried, I didn't see a problem with freezing, and I have an ordinary refrigerator-freezer, nothing special.

Alcohol-free wine and beer are available, or you can simmer the wine or beer for about ten minutes to remove the alcohol. If you know a home brewer, you can buy unfermented beer—and possibly also find a customer for your soap! You may find home brewers by searching online for home brew clubs in your area. Unfermented beer would have neither alcohol nor carbonation—excellent for soapmaking.

You *must* flatten *any* carbonated liquid you use for soapmaking, regardless of whether you freeze it. To flatten beer or sparkling wine, pour it into a container that leaves as much surface area as possible open to the air. Let it sit at room temperature for a day. Whipping it with a whisk may speed things up. Carbonation may also be removed by adding a pinch of baking powder, salt, sugar, or almost any other granular substance that you're willing to have in your soap. The liquid will foam up vigorously, then go flat.

Don't leave your beer or wine at room temperature for *too* long, or it will mold. Even covered, it picks up enough mold spores from somewhere—or maybe they're already there—to develop some impressive fungi. (Maybe I should have photographed my spectacular collection, but it was rather disgusting, and I decided to spare you.) Either cook it, flatten it with sugar or another granular ingredient, or just don't let it sit so long.

Lye dissolves a little more slowly in wine and beer than it does in water.

If you're sensitive to the ammonia-like fumes of milk soapmaking, be aware you may have the same reaction when beer or wine is the soapmaking liquid.

Beer and wine soap don't really retain the odor of the liquids. But they're not odorless, and the odor won't necessarily complement all fragrances. I avoid florals, in favor of wood, musk, or herbal scents. Of course, there are beer and wine fragrances as well, if that's what you want.

Overall, I preferred the beer soaps I made to the wine ones. My fear that the beer soap would smell like beer and leave me smelling like beer was unfounded. The beer soaps I made were quite good soap. I thought the wine soaps were more run-of-the-mill. I don't think wine hurts soap, particularly. But it did seem that beer helped it.

OCTOBER

Basic Beer Soap and Variations

9 ounces (255 grams) lard
4.5 ounces (128 grams) coconut oil
6 ounces (171 grams) grapeseed oil
10.5 ounces (298 grams) olive oil
9 ounces (255 grams) beer
2 teaspoons sugar
4.0 ounces (116 grams) lye

1. Combine the beer and the sugar. Stir until the beer stops foaming.
2. Let sit for a few hours or overnight. Freeze.
3. Melt the coconut oil and lard. Add to the grapeseed oil and olive oil.
4. If you're using a fragrance, add it to the oils.
5. Combine the lye with the frozen beer. Stir until the beer is melted and the lye is dissolved.
6. Add to the oil mixture. Proceed as for any cold process soap.

Two beer soaps. Color variations are caused by different fragrance oils. The lighter one is the basic recipe; the darker is the All-Veg Beer Soap from the next section.

Chocolate Ale Variation

Use ale for the liquid instead of beer. Remove the carbonation by adding 1 tablespoon of cocoa powder in addition to the sugar. Strain, freeze, and continue as for the basic recipe. Or instead of the sugar, add 1 to 1½ tablespoons of honey to the lard and coconut oil before heating. When it's all melted together, add to the liquid fats and stick blend to make sure the honey is well mixed.

Chocolate Ale Soap. The cocoa gives a speckled color, but not a grainy texture.

All-Veg Beer Soap

Victorian trade card showcasing Germany and German beer

You don't need to use lard to make a great beer soap. Here's a recipe with all vegetable fats.

        10.5 ounces (298 grams) sunflower oil
        10.5 ounces (298 grams) olive oil
        9 ounces (255 grams) coconut oil
        9 ounces (255 grams) flat beer, frozen
        4.2 ounces (121 grams) lye

Trying Wine in Soapmaking

Vintage wine label, 1930s

One of my most helpful hints is to try almost anything you want—in a two-bar batch. If you don't like it, you haven't lost much. If you do, scale it up. Here's a description of the process I used to formulate a wine soap.

I started by searching online for other people's experiences, and asking friends what they'd done with wine soap. My online search yielded a lot of opinions. I read many descriptions of instant trace and bad odors. Discussions of the color of red wine soap included descriptions ranging from red, pink, or other red shades, to beige, to gray.

Wine, of course, exists in many forms—soapmaking results may well have varied depending on the type used. I assumed that most soapmakers would be looking for inexpensive dry wine—not fine table wine, but not rotgut, either. I used inexpensive cabernet sauvignon and chardonnay—the kind of wine a restaurant might serve in carafes. The alcohol content of both was 12%. Sweet or fortified wines might get completely different results.

I strongly prefer freezing any liquid ingredients other than water—plus, I'd run into opinions that it's not possible to freeze wine without removing most or all of the alcohol. So, I cooked a large bottle of red wine to remove the alcohol and then froze the wine.

It worked in my soap, but I learned that removing the alcohol isn't important if you do freeze the wine—and that wine that contains alcohol *will* freeze.

Wine Soap Experiments and Recipes

The picture I've provided here below each recipe shows soap that was made with that recipe plus the wine it was made from. All the pictures were taken in the same location, and I've tried to standardize color to allow comparison.

Wine Soap #1

15 ounces (425 grams) grapeseed oil
6 ounces (171 grams) olive oil
9 ounces (255 grams) coconut oil
9 ounces (255 grams) dealcoholized, frozen red wine
4.1 ounces (118 grams) lye

My red wine had been reduced by 50% by simmering in a slow cooker for several hours. I used a red wine fragrance but didn't think the scent resembled red wine particularly—more like Concord grape juice. Trace was about average, possibly a little slow.

If I'd been aiming for a red color, I would have been disappointed—the color was tan, nearly caramel. I wondered if a less green oil mixture might have minimized the drift into the brown color range in the finished soap. So, I developed a second recipe with very pale fats.

Wine Soap #2

       9.9 ounces (281 grams) almond oil
       10.2 ounces (289 grams) avocado butter
       9.9 ounces (281 grams) coconut oil
       9 ounces (255 grams) dealcoholized, frozen red wine
       4.3 ounces (123 grams) lye

The soap remained a dull reddish color for about fifteen minutes after pouring, then changed to approximately the same color as the previous batch. An apparent failure of my idea that paler oils would solve the problem—but overnight, it faded to a pale beige with a slight pinkish cast. Still not red, but light enough that coloring or marbling with color would work.

You could go on with experiments like this—use red wine cut 50-50 with water. Use rosé wine. Or, unless you or your client definitely wants red wine in the soap, use white. Try cutting the wine 50-50 with milk. Or with coconut milk—that's whiter than dairy milk. You can lighten color with titanium dioxide, but it cuts lather, so I don't.

Also, you could skip the step that concentrates the wine—cooking the alcohol off. I found contradictory opinions when I asked around and read advice online. Some said dealcoholizing is necessary, some said it isn't. So, my next question was: What happens if you don't cook off the alcohol from the wine?

Wine Soap #3

I continued with the same recipe as for Wine Soap #1, but substituting white wine that had been frozen but not dealcoholized. I used white wine for a somewhat arbitrary, but practical, reason—I had cooked all the red. The alcohol content was the same. I could have bought more of the same type of red wine, but just for finding out if alcohol was a deal breaker in soapmaking, I saw no reason to do that.

The first question was whether full-alcohol wine would freeze at all. This turned out to be no problem, at least when doing it in ice cube trays.

The second question was whether the alcohol would accelerate trace. The soap in this experiment traced much more quickly than in the previous batches. It wasn't impossible to handle, though—just fast. Online accounts of instant trace may have referred to batches where the wine wasn't frozen, or where the wine had more sugar than the chardonnay I used. I'd say the same about reports that alcohol makes soap erupt in a "volcano," since there was no tendency to do that at all with frozen wine—the "volcano" soap must have been made with liquid wine.

My conclusion was that alcohol didn't accelerate trace to an unmanageable extent, but it did seem to accelerate. (See August for a number of ways to deal with accelerants.) I discussed this with a friend who has made many more batches of wine soap than I have. She says fast trace has been no problem at all for her, and she chalks that up to using oils that trace slowly, and to having considerable experience with wine soap. (She also uses the wine frozen.)

So, it's a possibility you might plan for in your experiments. Be ready to deal with fairly quick trace if it happens, but don't worry excessively about it.

I'd say dealcoholizing could serve a purpose, but it is optional. If your scent or base oils tend to accelerate, you might be well advised to remove from the picture any possible accelerating effect of alcohol. Otherwise, just have your molds ready and pay attention.

What Would I Do?

If I were making wine soap for sale, I'd experiment more to see whether removing alcohol makes a more emollient soap.

For wine soap, I'd use oils that would contribute as little as possible to color. For red wine soap, I'd use a natural or artificial colorant to get the red wine shade. I think buyers will expect the color to be similar to that of the wine, and I didn't find wine itself to be capable of producing a red color.

I'd also use a wine fragrance if I were making wine soap for sale.

Beer soap is far nicer than I imagined when I began these experiments. I'd probably test a few fragrances before I settled on one or two—a beer or ale fragrance? Spicy? Musky?

I might try beer as a liquid with 100% coconut oil soap superfatted at 20%. I'd expect some impressive lather with that one.

Of the various granular ingredients I used to flatten the beer, I preferred sugar.

Developing Your Own Recipes

I've made many kinds of soap, but when readers first asked about beer and wine soaps, I had no idea how to make them. With this project, then, it seemed a good time to go into the general way I learn about new kinds of soapmaking, and how I develop recipes—a subject I've always wanted to discuss.

It helps if you have experience with other people's soap recipes before you try inventing one. If you don't, you can still develop your own recipes, but be ready to practice a little patience.

Choosing Ingredients

When talking about lye calculators below, I discuss some of the practical issues in choosing fats. Besides those, though, there are esthetic decisions to make.

Almost all unrefined fats, and some specialty liquids, have an odor of their own. It's not usually a bad odor, though, and in many cases, it wears off as the soap cures. In my experience, unrefined shea butter, hemp oil, cocoa butter, neem oil, and wheat germ oil have odors of their own, as do all milk products, beer, wine, fruit juices, and many other liquids. With unrefined fats, it's probably best to assume there's some odor.

Color may be a consideration as well, especially with unrefined oils. Any natural or artificial colorant will have its color altered by the colors of oils in the soap, as well as by the color of any fragrance or essential oil. On the other hand, the colors of oils may not be the sole other source of a soap's final color, as we saw in the wine soap experiments above—liquids, including fragrances and water substitutes, contribute color, too.

When you choose olive oil, go by price. Cheapest is usually best for soapmaking. Cheaper olive oil has less flavor—which also means less odor. It also may be more acidic, which would promote saponification. I have not found pomace olive oil to be any better for soapmaking than ordinary olive oil. It used to be cheaper, but that has changed in many places, as demand has increased. If you want to minimize the green color, "light" olive oil or "Refined A" olive oil might be worth the extra cost—but I have yet to find an olive oil that's truly colorless.

You should test small batches before deciding to use a product in quantity. And give the soap a chance to cure before deciding. (Unrefined wheat germ oil, which smells like vitamin pills when fresh, completely loses its scent in a couple of weeks.)

If a fat or liquid retains some odor, you can choose a fragrance to complement it. For the most part, fat odors tend toward nutty, so a woody or musky fragrance would be a good pick. That also works well for beer and wine soap, and of course, there are ale, beer, and wine fragrances that enhance the natural scent, if that's what you want.

Using a Lye Calculator

You definitely need a good lye calculator. There is absolutely nothing difficult about using one. You enter your oil ingredients, and the calculator figures the lye and liquid. I've known aspiring soapmakers who were terribly put off and intimidated by the name, but lye calculators are a soapmaker's best friend.

I use SoapCalc. Take some time and read the information pages on the web site—there's a lot of good material there.

SoapCalc has the steps numbered in order, so you just follow along, one step at a time. Along the way, you can change its defaults to suit your technique. This is easy to do—just type in the values you want. I change the default value for "Water as % of oils" from 38% to 30%. If my liquid is water or milk, I use 8% superfatting rather than the default 5%. Otherwise, I stick with the superfatting default—when I haven't, I've gotten soaps that were too soft.

Next, you'll plug in the fats you plan to use, and the percentages you're considering. Unless you're making a single-oil soap, you're looking for a good blend.

Then you click on "Calculate Recipe" and get your results. You also get a "snapshot" of your finished soap, telling you what its properties will be. Here's an explanation of the properties and numbers you'll see.

Hardness—You want your soap hard enough that it unmolds and doesn't disappear quickly in use, but not so hard that it feels like a pebble when you try to wash with it. As a rule of thumb, a soap should contain one-third to two-thirds hard fats—fats with melting points above normal room temperature. At least one-third hard fats will almost always give you a soap that's in the normal range for hardness. If you want shaving soap, though, you might do better with a hardness value that's below the optimum range SoapCalc suggests. And in my book *Smart Soapmaking*, I have one recipe that contains 100% hard fats!

Cleansing—The cleansing number tells you how well the soap cleans. If your soap will be used for washing a mechanic's greasy hands, you want a fairly high cleansing number, maybe out of range. Facial soap for dry skin? Go in the other direction.

Conditioning—This measures how emollient the soap is. It's pretty much a matter of taste and use, so it's subjective. A soap with a high conditioning number will leave your skin feeling like you've used a light lotion—though you may not be satisfied with the cleansing. Quite a few fats, particularly solid ones, have good conditioning value—but if acne is a consideration, find out if a conditioning oil is comedogenic (acne-causing) before using it in a facial soap. (You can do this by searching online. Put the oil name in quotation marks and then add the word "comedogenic" *outside* of the quotes.)

Bubbly Lather—You probably want bubbly lather, especially if you're selling or gifting your soap, since most people are used to that. Usually the bubbly lather pops up first, as soon as the soap gets wet, followed by denser, creamy lather as you use the soap.

Bubbly lather comes mostly from coconut oil, palm kernel oil, and castor oil. These all have disadvantages along with that advantage. Coconut oil is drying and can cause acne. (Odd that it would do both, but that's the case.) Many soapmakers avoid palm products for environmental reasons, and palm kernel oil is also drying. Castor oil accelerates trace, and this may be a handful for an inexperienced soapmaker.

Bubbly lather can be increased by adding up to one teaspoon of sugar per pound of oils. For this month's basic recipe, I deliberately reduced the amount of coconut oil, counting on the natural sugars in the beer and wine, plus sugar added to flatten the bubbles, to bring the lather up to normal.

Another way to boost bubbly lather is to make your soap in a log mold and cut the bars with a crinkle cutter. This works because the "corrugated" faces have a greater surface area than a straight cut. Surprisingly, the corrugations last for most of the life of the soap as it's used.

Creamy Lather—In most soaps, this is the thick second lather you get when you've used the soap for a few seconds. In Castile soap, this is the *only* lather you'll get. Quite a few fats, both vegetable and animal, have good values for creamy lather.

Iodine—A low value for iodine indicates that the soap will probably be hard. (This is a value I haven't used much.)

INS—The INS value is related to the soap's hardness to some degree, but I use it mostly to give me a picture of how easily my mixture will saponify. A value around 160 is ideal, but numbers as low as 130 are quite workable. The low values of some single oils indicate their difficulty—olive oil, at 109, is notoriously difficult. My experiments with canola and other low-INS vegetable oils were just that—experiments that produced, with a great deal of difficulty, unusable soap.

SoapCalc helpfully gives the values for individual oils for all these characteristics. If your recipe comes up short in one or more category, add or substitute an oil that's strong in what your mixture is missing.

Once I have a recipe that looks good numerically—fits into all the "good" ranges for the above values—I figure it for both a tiny test batch and a larger, normal-size batch. SoapCalc makes this easy—just change the quantity before printing out a second time. I strongly recommend a small-scale experiment at the start of testing any recipe. My first run with a new recipe will be a batch of two bars, 7.5 ounces total oil weight.

A Few Final Tips

- It's not easy to make small batches with a stick blender. For my "experiment-size" batch, I use a countertop blender.
- For small batches, I recommend weighing in grams. It's more accurate.
- If you need to round a measurement, do so conservatively. For example, if your scale didn't measure in tenths of a unit, then you'd normally round to the next whole number for amounts .5 and above. However, I try to look at the whole picture. If I'm superfatting at 5%—which would be close to minimal—I'll probably round lye amounts slightly down or oil amounts slightly up. For example, if the lye amount prescribed by SoapCalc was 29.6 grams, and my scale wouldn't read tenths of a gram, I'd round down to 29 instead of up to the mathematically correct 30.
- As you make your experimental batch, take notes.
- Let the soap cure and test it before you decide to make a large batch of the recipe with no changes.

An Approach to Experimenting

Maybe instead of wanting to try a whole new formulation, you just have a specific question or two. For example, "Is it necessary to flatten beer and remove the alcohol before making soap?"

If that's the case, first do some research. In the case of beer and wine soap, I quickly found out—by asking a couple of chemist friends and searching online—that you absolutely do need to flatten beer or any other bubbly liquid before you make soap. The evidence was strong enough that I decided to accept it without testing. (I don't try absolutely everything, especially when it's sort of hazardous . . .)

That left the part about removing the alcohol. I knew I wanted to freeze the beer or wine to avoid scorching, but that alcohol lowers the temperature at which a liquid will freeze. I tried freezing some beer and wine *without* boiling it to remove alcohol. The beer froze, the wine didn't. I made soap with the beer and tried it. It didn't seem especially drying—but at this point, I'd recommend testing a few bars yourself and seeing how it works on your own skin. And if you're *selling* beer or wine soap, it might well be a good idea to boil off the alcohol just to be safe, or to use non-alcoholic beverages to begin with.

When you're looking for an answer to a specific question like this, it's very important to use a tried and true recipe for your experiments. Don't branch out into unfamiliar recipes until you've nailed down the way the ingredient in question will behave, or the effect the technique in question will produce. Just one wild card per experiment! That way, you'll get results you can use.

I often tell students that, when you experiment, the only thing you are guaranteed to get is information. True as that is, it's also possible to get information to the effect that you should have done more research before you tried something, or that you didn't set up your experiment very well. *Not* the information you want. Research first, then experiment in such a way that your results tell you what you want to know.

NOVEMBER
NATURAL COLORANTS
Pumpkin Pie Soap
Taming Soda Ash

Natural Colorants in Soapmaking—Why?

The main reason for using natural colorants is that they produce beautiful, subtle shades. Used correctly, these colors are stable.

Also, many soapmakers want to avoid dyes and artificial colors in their soaps. One of the reasons for making soap yourself to begin with is to avoid artificial ingredients. But supposing you want soap that isn't ivory-to-beige, you usually would have to color it with *something*.

Of course, most oils contribute some color—one of the prettiest soaps I ever made was a pale celadon green, the color being pure serendipity, the colors of the oils I used. So, oils can contribute color, as can liquids, if you use something other than water. And if you infuse one of your oils with herbs or flowers, that will affect the color as well. Finally, if you use essential oils or fragrance oils, they too may affect the color of the soap. Anything containing vanillin, for example, will slowly turn to a dark brown, and other fragrances have more subtle color.

But when we talk about natural colorants, most of the time, we're talking about natural ingredients that are used only for their color, or mostly for that. So: Ingredients other than the base oils, EO or FO, and liquids that are part of the soap formulation itself.

Like artificial colorants, strong natural colorants shouldn't be used too heavily, or you will get color that comes through in the lather and may even stain linens. For a more intense effect with less color, swirling or marbling may be a good choice.

However, not all natural colors are strong. Some fade almost to white before the soap even sets. Others turn out splotchy, grayed, or dull. One of my failures was soap I made with cranberry juice for liquid. It turned out an ugly grayish white—completely different from the color from orange or tomato juice, which both make a stable orange.

I read that liquid cochineal is a very strong color, and that "it doesn't take much." It didn't work that way for me. I added more and more, and more again, and after a few turns with my blender, the soap would be back to pale pink. Finally I had to pour it—and it faded even more as it cured. In the end, it was pure white. Possibly there was something wrong with the product I bought, but I couldn't find any other, so my cochineal experiment was not a success.

Some soapmakers do preliminary testing with a colorant, first in the oils they plan to use, then in a lye solution, and finally in a test batch of soap. That's probably a good idea, though I've never been that methodical.

One thing to remember in discussing natural colorants is that it's possible to use more than one at a time. So, if you want an apple-green shade, for example, the way to get it may be to mix green and yellow, rather than to look for a single natural colorant that will give you the exact shade you want.

Professional soapmakers who use natural colorants often opt to use only a few. They've worked out good technique for consistent results with these colors, and they stick with their tried-and-true methods and formulations. They're also likely to find a supplier whose products they like, and to continue to buy from that same vendor.

Using Natural Colorants in Soapmaking

When colorants are natural, that doesn't mean they aren't chemicals. Everything's a chemical, including our own bodies. Natural colorants can and do react with the lye, or with other ingredients in the soap.

Solid powders can be steeped in one of your base oils, or may be added to the soap at trace. Mix the powder with part of the base oil if you do add at trace, so you don't get lumps. Or mix it with some of the soap. (You'd start from light trace, if you do this, so you'll have enough time.) Powders can be scratchy if added at trace, so you'd have a scrubby soap. If your powder tends to irritate the skin, it may well be more irritating if added at trace than if it's infused in the base oils and sieved out.

I always freeze liquids other than water. If your main colorant is a liquid such as fruit juice, beer, or tea, I recommend freezing.

Plant-based colorants may morph in contact with lye, temporarily or permanently. Or the lye may destroy the color altogether—I was not successful with either cranberry juice or cochineal. Both soap batches lost the red color completely.

Mineral colorants are stable. What you see is pretty much what you get.

Results with some colorants may be inconsistent or uneven. Results may vary with products from different vendors.

If your color is too intense, you may get colored lather, and the soap may stain linens. Some colors, used in a higher concentration, are a nuisance to clean out of your bathtub.

Some natural colors are also used as dyes for fibers and other materials. Powders or oil infusions of these colors may stain your clothing or other absorbent surfaces.

Test the soaps critically with respect to lather and texture. The loveliest color in the world won't work if the soaps are scratchy or low-lathering.

Some soapmaking books tend to gloss over the fact that trial and error is part of everyone's process. That leaves many readers thinking they're the only ones who have to try several variations to get what they want. But all that is normal.

Colors, Oils, and Soap

The color of a soap comes from everything in it. If you're using a natural color that's the opposite of one of your oil colors, or if you mix two natural colors that are opposites, you'll get gray—or possibly brown, depending on which colors are used in what proportions.

Opposite colors are identified graphically in a traditional color wheel, such as shown above (courtesy of MarianSigler Images). To simplify and summarize:

- Red is the opposite of green.
- Yellow is the opposite of purple.
- Blue is the opposite of orange.

So, for example, if you're aiming for a pink or reddish soap, you'd think twice before using a strongly green olive oil. If you're making purple soap, you might prefer not to use a fragrance oil with a strong yellow hue.

I have two basic recipes in this lesson. One recipe contains olive oil, which may add color—greenish to beige—to soaps. If that would work well with your colorant, it's a good choice. The other recipe is about as flat white as it can be. Use this with colors that don't work well with green, like reds and oranges, or to maximize the brightness of natural colorants. (For more information about the effect of oil color on soap color, see October's wine soap experiments.)

Another consideration, if you're infusing color in one of your oils, is the percentage of that oil in the soap formulation. If your soap has a high percentage of that oil, you may wish to infuse only some of the oil with colorant and leave the rest without.

In the experiments described below, none of the soaps contain any fragrance or essential oil, or any other additives besides the colorant.

NOVEMBER

Plant-Based Colorants

Vegetable colorants include herbs, seeds, spices, and liquids such as juices, wine, beer, and coffee. Some plant-based colors are more stable than others, and it's a good idea to either research a plant product for soapmaking or start with a small experiment. Some plants produce surprising colors—not the color of the original material at all. Or it may be a variation of the original color—usually duller. Some plant colorants can be irritating to the skin if too much is added.

The range of colors is wide. I've experimented with many, but the possibilities are more or less endless. You can get color by steeping plant materials in your liquid, infusing your oil with them, using juice for your liquid, or adding them directly to the soap. If you do add them directly, you may use them to make the soap scrubby or exfoliant. Or you may make them as smooth as possible.

Natural colorants may not produce as even a result as you might get with artificial colors. However, for many of us, that's part of the charm. Some may fade more quickly than you'd like.

If you don't get good results adding a vegetable colorant to the liquid oils, try adding it when the soap is near trace. The effect of the lye will be somewhat reduced at that point—though it isn't eliminated.

There are hundreds of possibilities, far more than I can test. Here's a selection.

Teas and Other Liquids

You can make a tea out of any plant material that has water-soluble color in it. The procedure is the same as if you're making tea to drink: Pour hot or boiling water over the plant material, let it steep, and strain out the solids.

Other liquids may include fruit and vegetable juices, coffee, chocolate milk—almost any liquid that has a strong color of its own.

Liquids other than water may produce ammonia-like fumes. Have good ventilation!

Orange juice and peel used as coloring. The color of this soap held up well.

Oil Infusions

Annatto

Oils may be infused with solids such as spices, herbs, and powdered colorants such as annatto, alkanet, or madder root. In order for an oil infusion to work, at least some of the plant material's color must be oil soluble.

Some powders will make a usable infusion if you mix the oil and the powder and let them sit for a while, stirring occasionally. With others, heating the oil with the colorant is recommended to extract the color. Ask the vendor, or find out what has worked for others. Some colorants are affected by high pH, and with those, it's often best to add them at light trace. Mixing the powder with a little oil can help with color evenness and prevent speckles. Powdered colors added at trace may make the soap gritty, depending on how much you add.

NOVEMBER

With spices, the color you get in soap is pretty much what you'd expect from looking at the powder. The scent may survive saponification, too—so, if that's not what you want, it may be best to try a different colorant for the effect you want.

Spices are said to be skin irritants. However, soap itself is a skin irritant—as you know if you've ever failed to rinse it off! I'm sure that spice essential oils can concentrate this irritation, but I'm not sure powdered spices are actually likely to make much difference. If you're selling soap, though, you're well advised to tread carefully here. You have little or no control over how people use your product.

Dried herbs work better than fresh, in my experience—and I'm referring to *thoroughly* dried herbs, such as ones you'd buy for cooking. My efforts with fresh or casually home-dried herbs didn't turn out especially well. The infusion became cloudy, possibly moldy, before it changed color to any great degree.

The amount of colorant varies depending on how strong a color you want, but one teaspoon of powdered colorant per ounce of oil is a starting point. Strain the colorant out of the oil before you make soap.

I've had an unusually high amount of soda ash with spice-infused oils.

Soap made with annatto seed

Dry Colorants

Spices and other granular ingredients such as cocoa may be added dry. They're likely to give you a more intense color, and may also be more likely to irritate skin, compared to when infusing oil and straining it.

One way I've used powdered dry colorants is to blend them thoroughly in the oil before adding the lye mixture. Another is to mix the powder with a little oil and add at trace. This is one way to get around color morphing, if your colorant is sensitive to pH.

How much to use? It depends how strong you want the color to be—but many soapmakers start with one teaspoon of dry powdered colorant per pound of oils.

Another way to use dry colorant, if the powder is water soluble, is the "tea dye" method: Make a strong "tea" with the colorant, filter out the particles, and add it at trace. (See the madder root experiment below.) I call this "tea dye" because it's different from simply making a tea with the powder and replacing the liquid with it. With this method, your "tea" is so concentrated that it's actually a natural dye, and you're adding it when the lye has been mostly neutralized by the acids in the fats. This is very effective with colorants that react badly to high pH.

Other Plant Materials

Flecks of cucumber or citrus peel may be used for both color and texture. Coffee grounds can be added for a scrubby, somewhat deodorant kitchen soap.

Other Natural Colorants

Animal Product Colorants

Some natural colors come from animal products. Milk soap will turn brown if it's not chilled, and many people like the brown color. Cochineal is derived from insects.

Mineral Colorants

Clays of various kinds are mined and processed for soapmaking use. They can give a surprising array of colors, including green, orange, red, gold, pink, yellow, and white. The description the vendor gives should be enough to let you know exactly what to expect. Note, though, that clay does change the texture of soap. That's desirable for some soaps, especially shaving soap. But again, don't use too much, or the soap won't lather well.

Mineral colorants such as ultramarines and oxides aren't technically natural, since they're manufactured products. But they are replicates of naturally occurring minerals, artificially produced for purity.

Mineral colorants and clays are easy to use for creating swirls and other patterns, since they don't bleed.

Basic Colored Soap #1

This is my usual recipe for testing colorants, with 70% olive oil and 30% coconut oil. It's best to use with colorants that will work with a greenish or pale beige background color.

Test Batch Size

This makes two individual bars of soap. Making a tiny test batch like this is the way I start out with every new recipe. Weights are in grams only, because I don't recommend using ounce quantities for such small amounts—grams are more accurate, and accuracy is crucial when making small batches.

> 64 grams coconut oil
> 149 grams olive oil
> 64 grams liquid
> 30 grams lye

Full Batch Size

This is my typical 30-ounce batch. Still a small batch, about eight bars.

> 9 ounces (255 grams) coconut oil
> 21 ounces (595 grams) olive oil
> 9 ounces (255 grams) liquid
> 4.2 ounces (121 grams) lye

If the liquid I use is anything but water, I freeze it. If I'm using sugar, honey, or other water-soluble additives, I add them to the liquid before freezing. If I'm using botanicals, purees, grains, or anything else that's not water soluble, I add it to the oil mixture and blend well before adding the lye mixture.

Variations

Sage Soap—Expecting green, which is what other soapmakers had reported, I infused olive oil with commercial culinary dried sage, using the concentration recommended on several web sites that discussed natural colorants. Even after several weeks, the oil did not look different from ordinary olive oil. When the soap ingredients were combined, though, the mixture first turned bright red, then faded through salmon, khaki, tan, and beige, finally ending up pale green. A very nice color, but the process of getting there was quite startling.

Yarrow Soap—Made with the "tea dye" method. The night before I made the soap, I made a strong tea with yarrow powder. In the morning, I filtered it and set it aside. I withheld 20 grams of water from the 64 called for in my Test Batch Size formula (so only used 44 grams of water to dissolve the lye.) I made the soap otherwise per the recipe, and added 20 grams of the yarrow tea at trace. The result was a pale, clear yellow.

Cinnamon Soap—Warm brown, retained some cinnamon fragrance.

Cocoa Soap—Light brown, no chocolate fragrance. Sift the cocoa to eliminate lumps.

Coffee Soap—Tan, with speckles from added coffee grounds. I expected a darker color, since I used strong black coffee.

Turmeric Soap—And finally . . .

Basic Colored Soap #2

This soap is flat white before colorant is added. I test with this one when a colorant might be in conflict with the natural color of olive oil. Good for warm shades like red, orange, and yellow.

Test Batch Size

Makes two bars. As with Basic Colored Soap #1, weights are in grams only, because I don't recommend using ounce quantities for such small amounts.

    70 grams almond butter
    72 grams coconut oil
    70 grams almond oil
    64 grams liquid
    30 grams lye

Full Batch Size

    9.9 ounces (281 grams) almond butter
    9.9 ounces (281 grams) coconut oil
    10.2 ounces (289 grams) almond oil
    11.4 ounces (323 grams) liquid
    4.3 ounces (122 grams) lye

Variations

Paprika Soap—I did not find this soap irritating. However, I used it only on my hands, and I don't have sensitive skin.

Carrot Juice Soap—Carrot juice used for 100% of the liquid. Very strong fumes. Color faded from orange to pale yellowish tan as the soap cured.

Alkanet Root Soap Experiment

All soaps in this experiment were made with the recipe for Basic Colored Soap #1, as given earlier (with 70% olive oil, 30% coconut oil). The infused oil was reddish purple.

In the first batch, all the olive oil was infused oil. The soap was originally reddish purple, but it changed to deep navy blue as it cured. The soap was too dark, and the blue color also appeared in its lather. Usually, when this is the case, you'll stain linens when you use it—sometimes temporarily, sometimes not.

In the second batch of alkanet root soap, about a fourth of the olive oil was the infused olive oil, the rest was regular olive oil. The soap turned out dark pink.

I made one more batch with alkanet root, this time using very little of the infused oil. For about twelve hours, the soap was a bright gold ochre shade. After curing, it became golden pinkish beige.

Madder Root Soap Experiment

Dyer's Madder, from an old herbal

The first two soaps were made with the recipe for Basic Colored Soap #2, given earlier (with approximately equal proportions of almond butter, almond oil, and coconut oil). The infused oil was red. The only difference between the two batches was when the madder root was added. Infusing the almond oil with madder root before making the soap produced the gray soap on the left. Adding madder mixed with a little almond oil at trace produced the rose-colored soap on the right. Note the speckles in the second soap—many soapmakers complain that the undissolved powder makes the soap scratchy.

Two soaps made from the same recipe and colored with madder root

I made a third batch, using Basic Colored Soap #1, to see if I could get rid of the speckles. Madder root is soluble in water, so I made a strong "tea" with the madder and boiling water. I put the liquid through first a fine sieve, then a coffee filter. I held back some of the liquid when I dissolved my lye—12 grams out of the 64 I normally use for my test batch size. At trace, I added my madder "tea dye."

Success! The color was more of a peach shade than pink, probably because I used Basic Colored Soap #1, which has more color contribution from the oils. If I'd been aiming for a true pink, I would have used oils with as little color as possible, like the ones in Basic Colored Soap #2.

Madder root soap from "tea dye" method

How did I know madder root was soluble in water? I typed "Is madder root soluble in water" into my browser. Of course, another sure way to find out is to just try it and see if it works. If the powder is water-soluble, the water will be colored and stay like that, even after standing awhile. If the powder *isn't* water-soluble, it will sink to the bottom, leaving more or less clear liquid on top.

How did I know how much madder to use in the tea? I didn't. I used too much—in other words, more than the water could hold in solution. So, I wound up filtering out the excess.

How did I know how much tea to use in the soap? Again, I didn't. I tried what seemed like a reasonable amount, knowing that the color fades somewhat as the soap cures. If I hadn't liked the results, I would have used a different amount in another test batch. As it happened, I was happy with the result.

How much water can you safely withhold from the lye solution? *Theoretically*, you can dissolve 1 gram of lye in just .9 gram of water. I suspect you'd get fast trace with such a concentrated solution. The lowest proportion I've used in this method is about 1 gram lye to 1.5 grams water. I had no problems with that.

Pumpkin Pie Soap

9.9 ounces (281 grams) almond butter
9.9 ounces (281 grams) coconut oil
10.2 ounces (289 grams) almond oil
1.2 ounces (34 grams) pumpkin pie fragrance oil, or as recommended by vendor (optional)
11.4 ounces (323 grams) half and half (light cream), or yogurt mixed half and half with distilled water, or milk
1½ teaspoons sugar or honey
2 ounces (56 grams) pureed pumpkin
1 teaspoon pumpkin pie spice (optional)
4.3 ounces (122 grams) lye

1. Mix the half and half thoroughly with the sugar or honey. Melt the solid fats and add to the almond oil. Add fragrance, if using.

2. Combine lye with frozen ingredients. When all the lye is dissolved, add to the oils and blend nearly to trace.

3. Add the pumpkin puree and spice, if using.

I recommend tray molds or individual molds for any soap that contains milk.

Pumpkin pie fragrance will likely turn the soap brown, as it probably contains vanilla. Avoid it if you want an orange color.

If you want the soap to be *more* orange, consider using carrot juice, orange juice, powdered orange peel, or another orange colorant in addition to the pumpkin.

What Would I Do?

Before I tried natural colors, I imagined they would be less interesting and less stable than they turned out to be. As a general rule, I don't color soaps at all—but if I wanted to, I'd now try natural colorants in preference to anything else.

But you do have to work out the best technique for a particular colorant. If you want a particular natural color, spend time on research and experimenting. Test on a very small level before committing to a final formulation and technique.

If you don't get good results with one technique, try another. Adding the color at trace—whether in oil or in water—often alters the results dramatically.

Taming the Soda Ash Monster

What Causes Soda Ash?

I must have heard dozens of theories about the reason for soda ash. Here are some I remember.
- It happens mostly with high sugar soaps, like milk soap.
- It happens when there's some kind of disturbance in the natural temperature cycle of saponification and curing.
- It's caused by weather and atmospheric conditions.
- It's caused by air contacting the soap.
- It's a chemical reaction caused by specific ingredients.
- It's caused by pouring at thin trace.
- It's associated with particular oils.
- It's caused by unmolding the soap too soon.
- It's completely random.

Which is true? I've had experiences that support every one of these theories. And experiences that would seem to disprove most of them. The most bizarre experience I know of didn't happen to me, but to a friend, who I know is a good soapmaker. She made a batch of soap and poured into two molds, which were handled identically. One got soda ash, the other didn't.

What Prevents Soda Ash?

I've probably heard dozens of theories about *preventing* soda ash, as well.
- Spread plastic wrap across the surface of the soap. (I've advised this myself.)
- Put the soap mold in a closed box or bag after pouring.

- Insulate the soap.
- Spray the top with 92% alcohol after pouring.
- Avoid particular ingredients.
- Avoid soapmaking during particular weather conditions.
- Humidify the soap or the air around it while it's curing.
- Use hot process. From what I've heard, HP soap doesn't get soda ash.
- Use sodium lactate in your soap formulation.
- Use beeswax in your soap formulation.

The problem is, unless you do a double test, using a particular prevention method on different bars from the same batch, you have no idea whether the absence of soda ash proves anything. It's like the joke about the man who snaps his fingers to keep elephants away—he's sure it works, because there aren't any elephants nearby.

And if you actually do find a method that seems to prevent soda ash, you'd have to repeat it over a number of tests before you could say it worked.

Plastic wrap *has* worked well enough for me that I still recommend it, though I know it doesn't *always* work. People who have problems with it may sometimes be under the impression that the wrap has to be applied the second the soap is poured. I've had just as much success when I've waited a few minutes until the surface is stable. I've had evidence that it works, in that I've sometimes gotten soda ash where there's a wrinkle in the wrap and nowhere else.

On the other hand, I've also gotten soda ash on soap that was well covered. And once, with a batch colored with annatto seed, I got it on all six faces of the bars—which certainly suggests a lot more going on than simple air contact.

Alcohol didn't prevent the soda ash deposit—it just left the top of the soap oddly marked by the drops of alcohol spray. Maybe I used too much. The results weren't good enough for me to try again.

I've never done a double test using a closed box or bag. But I *have* tried this method with many soaps, and it has been quite rare for the bars to get soda ash. However, since I didn't use the method scientifically—with a "control" that didn't receive the treatment—I don't know whether the enclosure was the reason for the absence of soda ash. And a few bars *have* gotten soda ash when treated this way—so it's not a magic bullet.

One way to keep soda ash from being a *problem* is to use a log mold and to trim any surfaces you don't like. Obviously, this doesn't prevent soda ash from forming—it just skirts the problem altogether.

My Two Cents

So, you've got soda ash, regardless of any preventive measures you may have taken. Old advice was to rub the soap with alcohol—but although this removes the deposit, it also makes the soap look used, rendering it unsalable.

You can get surprisingly good results—at least with some soaps—by dunking the bar in water without rubbing it. This might not work for soaps with detailed patterns on the surface, though. I imagine they'd blur and look used.

I've gotten my best results with steam, and I've bought a clothing steamer for the purpose. It's quite surprising how little it takes. However, a friend says she got poor results with her steam iron, so it's still something of an open question.

Working around soda ash is a bit like trying to get through a maze blindfolded. I think it may have more than one cause, and more than one solution.

DECEMBER

WOOD SOAPS
Soap Gifts
Shaving Soap
Home Fragrancing

Wood Scents in Soapmaking—Why?

Wood scents and other wood ingredients have a long history in the perfumer's and soapmaker's repertoire. Wood scents such as pine and fir have long been popular with men, especially in the days when a more "perfumed" kind of soap might have been unacceptable to many of them. Sandalwood is a classic favorite of both men and women.

The old-fashioned pine tar soap has been used for many years for cleansing and deodorizing, and is believed by some to be helpful for certain skin conditions. (However, if you sell pine tar soap, do not make medical claims for it!)

Evergreen fragrances are also a staple of holiday home fragrancing and gift items.

An Avon soap from the 1950s. With its mild evergreen fragrance, it was marketed as a gift for men.

Evergreen and Other Tree Essential Oils

Here are some of the "woody" essential oils you can use in soap.

Juniper Berry—Fresh, clean, and somewhat spicy. The essential oil itself didn't seem to me to have a typical "Christmas tree" scent, but once I soaped it, it did. Does not accelerate trace.

Fir Needle—"Christmas tree" scent. It's sometimes reported to accelerate trace, but in my experiments, it didn't.

Balsam Peru—The scent is sweet, but medicinal. Probably better as a blending scent than for solo use. Definitely not a holiday evergreen scent.

Bay Leaf—Smells exactly like culinary bay leaf. This essential oil is a *very* strong trace accelerant, and few vendors say so. See August for suggestions for working with accelerants.

Eucalyptus—This is a "spa soap" smell, clean but not sweet. May remind some people of cold remedies. It does not accelerate trace.

Cedar Wood—A fresh, somewhat sweet scent, quite unlike the "cedar closet" odor I was expecting. Would blend well with orange. Does not accelerate.

White Birch—Said to have medicinal properties. It wasn't available from the soapmaking supply vendors I checked, so I wasn't able to test it. I've read that it accelerates trace.

Rosewood—Not recommended for environmental reasons, and may be an irritant as well.

Pine—Best used in combination with other scents. By itself, pine may be too much like the odor of commercial cleaners.

Sandalwood EO vs. FO— Is the Difference Worth the Cost?

Sandalwood essential oil is very, very expensive. So expensive that putting it into soap is probably out of the question. Fragrance oils are available, and some are advertised to be close to the real thing.

I bought a very small amount of sandalwood essential oil and several sandalwood fragrance oils. I liked the fragrance oils—they were good quality, and about what I expected in a sandalwood fragrance. So, I was hoping to be able to report that sandalwood essential oil is not sufficiently better to be worth considering.

However, now that I've tried both, I can't say that. The essential oil was far superior to the fragrance oil. There was almost no comparison. In addition to the expected scent, the essential oil had a fresh-cut wood note, almost a green aroma. It was amazing.

I would still not put sandalwood essential oil into soap. The fresh scent might be lost, and the cost would be staggering. I'm thinking it might work well in a very small quantity of solid perfume. Or at my wildest extravagance, in one bottle of lotion.

Basic Wood Soap and Variations

All the fats in this recipe are easily available from most grocery stores. Sugar will increase lather, but it's not necessary. If you use it, dissolve it in the water before adding the lye.

    21 ounces (595 grams) grapeseed oil
    9 ounces (255 grams) coconut oil
    2 ounces (56 grams) fragrance oil or essential oil, or per
        vendor's recommendation
    9 ounces (255 grams) water
    2 teaspoons sugar, optional
    4.1 ounces (117 grams) lye

Variations—Substitute milk, cream, yogurt mixed 50-50 with distilled water, flattened beer, or orange juice for the water. Any of these should be frozen in cubes before being combined with lye.

Soaps from the Past—Pine Tar Soap

Pine tar is used in many industries, including wood preservation, veterinary care, and the rubber industry as a solvent. Pine tar soap has been made for over a century and is still available today. I often get requests for recipes for it. It is said to be effective for some skin ailments, although the US Food and Drug Administration does not acknowledge it as medically effective.

Pine tar soap has a reputation for being difficult. This is because pine tar is a fairly strong trace accelerant. Reports are common of "soap on a stick" and having to cram the fast-solidifying stuff into molds.

Unscented, the soap does not smell like pine, or like tar. I can only describe it as "medicinal," maybe slightly metallic. If it's not to your taste, you may like it better if you add fir needle EO or other evergreen scent. Pine tar has a strong scent to overcome, so consult your fragrance vendor for upper limit amounts of FO or EO to add.

The soap is brown, but the lather is white.

Easy Pine Tar Soap

Pine tar soap is quite easy with this recipe. The selection of fats is designed to be chemically "slow," the low temperature helps keep the soap from accelerating, the recipe contains a little more water than usual, and the soap is already in the mold when you add the pine tar.

Pine tar is messy, so as much as possible, use cups, spoons, and other utensils that are disposable. I covered my work counter with newspaper to minimize cleanup.

You'll need a silicone loaf pan to make this. It should hold over a quart. The soap is about a quart of liquid, but you need extra space for stirring. Put the soap on a tray or other flat, solid surface before you begin. It's best if this "trivet" has a raised edge in case some of the soap spills over while you're stirring. The pan may retain the smell of pine tar and not be usable for other soaps—I used one I found at a thrift store.

7.2 ounces (204 grams) lard
9 ounces (255 grams) coconut oil
6 ounces (170 grams) almond oil
6 ounces (170 grams) olive oil
10.2 ounces (289 grams) water
1 tablespoon sugar
Optional fragrance (See note below.)
4.1 ounces (118 grams) lye
1.8 ounces (51 grams) creosote-free liquid pine tar

1. Dissolve the sugar in the water. Freeze in cubes.
2. Melt the lard and coconut oil together. Add the almond oil and olive oil.
3. Add the lye to the frozen sugar water. When the ice is melted and the lye is completely dissolved, add to the oil mixture.
4. Stick blend to very light trace. Pour into the mold.
5. Quickly stir the pine tar into the soap in the mold. Thoroughly work it into the corners and edges, stirring until well mixed. By this time the soap will be at heavy trace.
6. Let the mold sit until the soap is solid. Slice and let cure.

What Would I Do?

If I were going to make pine tar soap again, I would use an ounce or more of fragrance per pound of oils, and I would choose something strong.

Fragrances and Essential Oils for Gift Soaps

Unless you know someone's taste in fragrance, it's best to pick something that almost everyone likes. Based on vendors' lists of bestselling scents, here are a few suggestions.

Essential Oils
Lavender
Mint
Lemongrass

Fragrance Oils
Lemon
Vanilla
Almond
Mixed herbs
Oatmeal, milk, and honey
Holiday fragrances

Holiday Fragrance Oils

Every year brings a new crop of fragrance oils for the holidays. Some are evergreen fragrances, others are based on traditional holiday foods. The evergreen types can be especially welcome as a home fragrance if your Christmas tree is artificial. (See the discussion of home fragrancing, below.)

I'm more wary of most of the food ones. Of course it's a matter of taste, but most "cranberry" fragrances smell like red lollipops to me. Others, billed as eggnog, chestnut, or other holiday desserts, seem more akin to baby powder or floral.

"Snow" fragrances usually remind me of laundry detergent.

Chocolate, vanilla, and cinnamon are usually good choices, and mixed fruit and spice can work well, too. Many of these fragrances will turn the soap dark brown—so if that matters to you, ask the vendor if the fragrance discolors.

Gift Soap in a Hurry

Melt and Pour

There are excellent brands of melt and pour soap base, but I've never seen the good ones for sale in a craft store. I wouldn't give craft store melt and pour soap as a gift—it has very low lather, so the soap will be disappointing. You might be able to boost that lather by adding sugar—it's worth an experiment, if you're really stuck. Or, if you're really pushed for a gift and want it to be soap, some of the online vendors with good soap base will do express shipping for an extra fee.

There's no curing time for melt and pour, so the soaps will be ready almost immediately.

CPOP

One problem with making soap gifts can be that there's not enough time left for the soap to cure. Hot process is one answer to that, and another is "cold process oven process," or CPOP. For CPOP, you make cold process soap in molds that can withstand higher temperatures. I've used wood, which is safe in this range, and also silicone.

Right after pouring the soap, cover the mold with an oven-proof lid—not aluminum foil—and put it in a warm oven. The temperature should be around 170°F (around 75°C) or even lower—in fact, as low as your oven control will permit. (Mine goes down to 100°F, and that works fine.) Leave for a couple of hours. Test the pH when the soap cools, and don't give it to anyone until the pH has dropped to 9 or 10. (In my own tests, the soap reached a good pH right away, and came out of the molds cleanly as soon as it cooled.)

Even when the pH is good, the soaps last longer if they're not used for a week or two. For that time, store them on edge in a warm, dry place—preferably on a rack—to help some of the water evaporate.

It's best to do CPOP with the soap in a block or log mold rather than in individual molds. Surfaces of CPOP soap may not be smooth, and with a log mold, you can trim off anything you don't like. Slice the soap as soon as it's firm enough—being divided into individual bars will help it dry.

Packaging Soaps for Gifts

There are so many ways to package soap as an attractive gift. Here are a few.

- Fill a small basket with soap. Raffia makes a good basket filler, and you can create a finished appearance with clear basket wrap. All these things are easy to find at craft stores. Sometimes, you can find beautiful baskets at farmers markets or art fairs.
- Package soaps in small cellophane or fabric bags or fabric boxes. Net bags sold for wedding favors are easy and attractive, and they increase the soap lather, too.
- Package soaps with other toiletries such as bath crystals, lotion, or hand cream with the same fragrance.
- Add accessories such as loofah or mesh soap saver pouches, wood or plastic soap savers, a handknit washcloth, or a new or vintage soap dish. Nut, candy, and trinket dishes also make good soap dishes, combined with a soap saver.
- Make your own labels using clip art.

Use your imagination to complement your soaps with pretty packaging!

Juniper soap with fabric bag

Left: Soap with soap saver bag. Right: Soap paired with a collectible soap dish in a holiday theme.

From left to right:
1. Two soap savers, plastic and wood. The plastic ones work better, but the wood ones are more attractive. I always give them with handcrafted soap, because it lasts much longer if a soap saver is used.
2. Bazaar item, a soap holder made by folding a washcloth from both sides toward the center, wrapping it around a bar of soap, securing it at the neck with a clear rubber band, and adding trim. Clear rubber bands are sold in drugstores and grocery stores, along with other hair ornaments and bands.
3. Container with a jar of cream, a handknit washcloth, a bar of soap, and a bath pouf. The clear tube is a reused container that originally held cable ties.

Giving a Soapmaking Lesson

If the gift recipient is someone who's interested in handmade soap, why not teach them how to make their own? Assemble a starter kit of supplies, tuck in a gift card for the lesson, and teach your friend how it's done. It's an unforgettable gift.

Shaving Soap

Fans of shaving with handmade shaving soap say they get a smoother, longer-lasting shave. Shaving soap makes a unique gift, and you can easily find shaving mugs and brushes to go with it. (Shaving brushes are made from badger or boar hair, or with synthetic bristles.)

Shaving soap can be made in bars or can be poured directly into mugs. Any mug will do, but mugs intended especially for shaving soap make the gift extra special. Bar soap can be cut into chunks before placing in a mug.

Vintage shaving mug

If you use beer for your liquid, you MUST remove the carbonation. To flatten beer, pour it into a shallow container to expose maximum surface area. Let it sit at room temperature for a day. Whipping it with a whisk may speed things up. Carbonation may also be removed by adding a pinch of baking powder, salt, sugar, or almost any other granular substance you're willing to have in your soap. The liquid will foam up vigorously, then go flat.

Bentonite clay provides slip for the razor, so it's very common to include it in shaving soap.

If your mug can stand heat, you can CPOP the soap right in the mug.

If you make shaving soap for someone who hasn't tried it before, there are great videos they can view online about how to use a shaving mug and brush for the best lather and skin conditioning.

Deluxe Shaving Soap

10.5 ounces (298 grams) almond oil
5 ounces (142 grams) wheat germ oil
1.5 ounces (43 grams) castor oil
1.5 ounces (43 grams) aloe vera extract
10 ounces (284 grams) shea butter
1.5 ounces (43 grams) hemp butter
1½ tablespoons bentonite clay
Optional fragrance (See note.)
9 ounces (255 grams) water, milk, or beer
2 teaspoons sugar
3.8 ounces (108 grams) lye

1. Prepare the liquid by mixing water, milk, or flattened beer with sugar. Freeze in cubes.
2. Melt solid fats and combine with liquid fats, aloe vera extract, and bentonite clay.
3. Combine frozen liquid with lye. When liquid is thawed and lye is dissolved, pour through sieve into fats. Stir or stick blend to trace.
4. Pour into mugs or other molds. If you use mugs, don't fill to the brim—leave about an inch at the top for developing lather with the brush.

Note: Since shaving soap is used on the face, I recommend using less scent than you might for hand soap. Normally, I'd use up to two ounces of FO or EO in a batch this size, depending on the vendor's recommendation. For shaving soap, I'd use no more than half that. Many users prefer an unscented soap for shaving.

Simpler Shaving Soap

Use any soap recipe that has good creamy *and* bubbly lather—you need both. For each pound of oils, add one teaspoon of sugar and, if you can, two teaspoons of bentonite clay.

DECEMBER

Home Fragrancing

Since you already have supplies for adding scents to soap, why not do something more with them—and try other fragrancing ideas as well?

Holidays are enhanced by indoor scents—the smell of cooking, as well as traditional pine, orange, and spice scents. There are many ways you can add to them!

Also, if you have an artificial Christmas tree, you'll probably miss the scent of a natural one. You can buy ornaments that include scent, but why not make your own?

Potpourri

Dry—Making your own dry potpourri from scratch is a real art, and you need access to large amounts of fresh flowers. You also need a fragrance fixative, such as orris root. I've bought top quality lavender buds and left them in bowls with no fixative. The scent faded much too quickly, even when I "refreshed" the buds with lavender essential oil.

Simmering—You can make simmering potpourri from flowers, spices, or fruit. If it's on the stove, it has to be monitored well, or you risk it boiling dry. An electric mini slow cooker is probably safer, though you do have to pay attention to those as well. I experimented with a mixture of pumpkin pie spice, culinary orange oil, and hot water, with good results. The scent worked its way slowly through the house, and was mild and pleasant. I refreshed the hot water from time to time and scraped down the sides of the crock.

Antique potpourri bowls are often shallow and wide, which maximizes the surface area of the contents. They usually have tops, and sometimes a stirring tool as well. Some are elaborate urns—now very valuable antiques.

Reed Diffusers

In my experience, these provide scent to only a small area. The reeds have to be turned every few days, or they dry out and stop diffusing. Eventually, they dry up altogether, but you can get new ones without buying more scent. Some recipes call for diluting the fragrance oil with mineral oil or glycerine. Since both are more viscous than fragrance oils and essential oils, I don't see any reason to believe that would help.

Electric Warmers

There are electric potpourri warmers, as well as devices for melting scented wax pastilles. Almost any warmer that can be used safely would be effective. For example, I've seen recipes for half-pint mason jars filled with fragrant mixtures and placed on a mug warmer. Whatever you use, do it in accordance with manufacturer's directions and monitor for safety.

Candles

I don't make candles, and I've found that most scented candles I've tried don't really give much scent. There are exceptions, but I've had difficulty finding anything I like. Candles that seem quite fragrant in the store just don't burn with enough fragrance to make a difference. Others say that scented candles irritate their eyes.

Terrycloth

Cotton terrycloth—the old kind, not the velvety kind—consists of hundreds of tiny wicks. It diffuses scents very well. I use it for fragrancing in the bathroom and kitchen. Just put a few dabs of essential oil or fragrance oil on a cotton terry washcloth or bar mop towel and hang it over a towel rod. The scent doesn't carry far, but it's quite enough for a small room and lasts for days.

A pillow or other decorative object made of terrycloth could work in other rooms. For instance, a friend made a small pillow for me out of a holiday fingertip towel. If I set it under my Christmas tree with a dab of fir essential oil on it, it should scent the air around the artificial tree. A variation on this might be to make a patchwork tree skirt from heavy fabrics, including some terrycloth, and put the scent on those patches.

Choose a cloth color that won't show the discoloration of the oil.

Terrycloth fragrance pillow

Tea Ball

You can make a scent diffuser with a mesh tea ball. Soak several cotton balls in essential oil or fragrance oil, put them in the tea ball, and hang where you like. I tried it with a very large tea ball, and it works fairly well. Whether this could be made to look decorative is another question. The mesh would have to remain open for it to work, so it may be more appropriate in a bathroom or closet than hanging in an entryway.

Air Freshener

You can make gel-type air fresheners with ordinary gelatin, water, fragrance, and salt. (The salt is supposed to prevent mold.)

Orange Pomander Ball

The orange is completely studded with whole cloves. The secret here seems to be to use an icepick to make the holes, rather than trying to push the cloves in with your fingers. Also to roll the finished pomander ball in orris root powder, and to keep it in orris root, rolling it daily, in a cool dry place for several days. Some crafters kept the pomander in the refrigerator for this step. And then, you hang it rather than let it sit in a bowl, which apparently promotes mold.

I found that a pomander works very well in a small space like a coat closet, but a single one isn't noticeable in an average-size room.

Orange pomander ball

Other Possibilities

I've come across far too many ideas to try. You'll find dozens if you put the words "home fragrancing" into your browser.

www.ingramcontent.com/pod-product-compliance
Lightning Source LLC
Chambersburg PA
CBHW061140230426
43663CB00027B/2985